Cambridge English

Compact
First for Schools
Second Edition

Teacher's Book

Barbara Thomas

Laura Matthews

Cambridge University Press
www.cambridge.org/elt

Cambridge Assessment English
www.cambridgeenglish.org

Information on this title: www.cambridge.org/9781107415676

First published 2013
Second edition 2014
Reprinted 2018

Printed in Italy by Rotolito S.p.A.

A catalogue record for this publication is available from the British Library

ISBN 978-1-107-41556-0 Student's Book without answers with CD-ROM
ISBN 978-1-107-41560-7 Student's Book with answers with CD-ROM
ISBN 978-1-107-41567-6 Teacher's Book
ISBN 978-1-107-41577-5 Workbook without answers with Audio
ISBN 978-1-107-41572-0 Workbook with answers with Audio
ISBN 978-1-107-41558-4 Student's Pack (Student's Book without answers with CD-ROM
and Workbook without answers with Audio)
ISBN 978-1-107-41574-4 Class Audio CD
ISBN 978-1-107-41831-8 Presentation Plus DVD-ROM

Additional resources for this publication at www.cambridge.org/compactfirstforschools2

Contents

Map of the units

Unit	Topics	Grammar	Vocabulary	Writing
1 Family and friends	Family celebrations Friends	Present and future tenses State verbs Comparisons	Words often confused Matching expressions with similar meanings	Part 1: Essay understanding the question, paragraphing, linking words and phrases
2 Exploring the world	Adventure and travel Where you live	Past tenses Prepositions of time Adverb formation	Word building (1): adjective suffixes (-*able*, -*al*, -*ous*) Cities, towns and villages	Part 2: Story sequencing, using a range of past tenses, adjectives and adverbs
3 The entertainment industry	Films Music	Linking words and phrases The passive	Film and cinema Music	Part 2: Review organising paragraphs, recommending, using linking words and phrases
4 Active life	Sports Keeping fit and healthy	Modal verbs Prepositions following verbs and adjectives	Sports Food Word building (2): noun suffixes (-*ence*, -*ity*, -(*s/t*)*ion*)	Part 2: Letter and email giving advice, making suggestions, persuading, beginnings and endings
5 Learning	Ambitions and achievements Education	Conditionals	Phrasal verbs Careers Education	Part 2: Set text characters, events, types of question
6 Natural world	Environment and weather Wildlife	Countable and uncountable nouns Articles *so* and *such* (*a/an*), *too* and *enough*	Climate Environmental problems Animals	Part 2: Article keeping the reader's attention, describing and linking
7 People and style	Shopping and fashion People and feelings	Verbs and expressions followed by *to*-infinitive or -*ing* form Reported speech	Clothes Shopping Feelings	Part 2: Letter and email giving information, using linking words and phrases
8 Keeping up to date	Science Technology	Relative clauses	Science Computers Word building (3): prefixes and suffixes	Part 1: Essay planning, introductions and conclusions, using a range of vocabulary

Reading and Use of English		Listening	Speaking
Part 5: multiple-choice questions	Part 1: multiple-choice cloze	Part 3: multiple matching	Part 1: leisure activities Part 2: comparing ways of spending free time
Part 6: gapped text	Part 2: open cloze Part 3: word formation	Part 1: multiple-choice questions + short recordings	Part 3: discussing preferences, agreeing and disagreeing Part 4: talking about where you live
Part 7: multiple matching	Part 4: key word transformations	Part 4: multiple-choice questions + long recording	Part 1: adding extra information and comments Part 2: talking about films and music, avoiding unknown words, giving preferences
Part 5: multiple-choice questions	Part 2: open cloze Part 3: word formation	Part 2: sentence completion	Part 3: asking for opinions and reacting to opinions Part 4: discussing sports and keeping fit
Part 7: multiple matching	Part 1: multiple-choice cloze Part 4: key word transformations	Part 2: sentence completion	Part 1: discussing ambitions, achievements and education Part 2: making guesses
Part 6: gapped text	Part 2: open cloze	Part 4: multiple-choice questions + long recording	Part 3: agreeing, disagreeing, making a comment or suggestion Part 4: discussing ways of helping the environment
Part 5: multiple-choice questions	Part 4: key word transformations	Part 3: multiple matching	Part 1: expressing likes and dislikes Part 2: comparing different ways of shopping
Part 7: multiple matching	Part 3: word formation	Part 1: multiple-choice questions + short recordings	Part 3: structuring a conversation Part 4: discussing technology

1 Family and friends

Unit objectives

FIRST FOR SCHOOLS TOPICS	relationships, family
GRAMMAR	review of present and future tenses, comparisons
VOCABULARY	words often confused, matching expressions with similar meanings
READING AND USE OF ENGLISH	Part 1: meaning and grammar; Part 5: focus of different questions
WRITING	Part 1 essay: giving opinions and reasons
LISTENING	Part 3: listening for general meaning and details
SPEAKING	Part 1: answering questions about daily life Part 2: comparing photographs

Family celebrations

Listening

Part 3

1 Talk about what is happening in the photos with the whole class, e.g. what they think the people are celebrating, how the people are related, whether they are all enjoying themselves, whether these kinds of occasions are always fun.

2 Ask students to work in pairs to talk about their own family celebrations. When they've finished, ask a couple of pairs to tell the class what they talked about. Summarise any useful vocabulary as these kinds of photographs are common in Speaking Part 2.

3 🎧 02 Tell students to listen for the answers to the questions.

> **Answers**
> 1 Emily's family always have a party on New Year's Eve. It's well organised.
> 2 They went to a restaurant this year. Everything went well.
> 3 Nobody disagreed.

Recording script

Emily: On New Year's Eve, my family always get together and last year my uncle and his family came over from New Zealand. My mum always plans a party way in advance – she likes cooking and she's really good at organising all the games and everything. Everyone leaves it to her now as she's best at it but my uncle was ahead of her this time and he suggested we should all go out to eat. We'd never thought of doing that, well, just because we never have, but it was fun and everything went smoothly. Everyone agreed though that we really like our traditions so we'll celebrate at home again next year.

---

4 🎧 02 Ask students to look at A–F and decide which one matches what Emily said. Play the recording again so they can check their answers. Go through the options A–F and talk about why each one is wrong. See explanations below.

> **Answers**
> E There was a change of plan (*we'd never thought of doing that*) and it was successful (*it was fun and everything went smoothly*). Point out that this tests both understanding of the whole recording (that they changed their plan) and also a detail (it was successful). See Exam tip.
>
> A There is nothing to suggest that it was less well organised than usual.
> B Going out to eat was a change but it wasn't an unexpected event as it was planned in advance.
> C There is nothing to say it lasted longer than usual.
> D There was no difference of opinion (everyone agreed).
> F There is nothing to suggest that the day started off badly.

Exam task

🎧 03 Students have already matched Emily to E. Now they will hear three more speakers to match to the list A–F. Two of the statements don't match any of the speakers. Play the recording twice.

Go through the answers asking students why they chose them – ask them what they remember the person saying. Point out in the exam there will be eight (A–H) rather than six statements to match as here and five speakers rather than four. There will always be three statements which don't match any of the speakers.

> **Answers**
> Speaker 1 D
> Speaker 2 B
> Speaker 3 C
> **Speaker 1** Check they understand what *that didn't go down well* means. If they don't understand, it is explained in the next sentence – that the aunties were unhappy with the idea. But this isn't the same as F (the disagreement was before the day not on the day). Ask students why they didn't choose B or E (everything was the same as usual in the end).
> **Speaker 2** The answer is found in *the weird thing was that this time there was someone making a film on the beach and they asked us to be in the background*. Ask students why A is wrong (it's never very well organised and that didn't change this year).
> **Speaker 3** The answer is found in *Usually my grandparents and the others go home when it gets dark but this year was a bit different … When it got dark nobody moved and we carried on …* Ask students why B and E are wrong (they stayed longer than usual but there was no unexpected event or change of plan).

Recording script

You will hear three people talking about a family celebration. Choose from the list A–F what each speaker says about the celebration.

Speaker 1

My granddad's birthday is on Midsummer Day and the whole family meet up and have a picnic. When my cousins and I were

---

6   Unit 1   Family and friends

small we loved it, but now we've all got things we do, like I'm in a football team and my cousin has a job in a café. So we suggested we had the party at home instead this year but <u>that didn't go down well.</u> My parents were OK with it but my aunties said it would upset granddad and all the plans were already made, so I had to miss my football match and the team lost – probably not because of me but you never know.

Speaker 2

My cousins live in the city and visit us twice a year. There's never any discussion about what we'll do when they arrive. We pile the cars up with loads of stuff and head down to the beach where we have a huge barbecue. Then everyone does what they want – sit and read or play games or swim or whatever. It's usually a really quiet place but <u>the weird thing was that this time there was someone making a film on the beach and they asked us to be in the background.</u> We didn't mind because we just carried on with what we were doing anyway.

Speaker 3

The first of May is a holiday and my family always have a big meal together at home. Usually the weather is nice and we eat outside. We always play the same games and eat the same food and everybody knows what to expect. <u>Usually my grandparents and the others go home when it gets dark but this year was different</u> because my uncle has a new job in Brazil and he and my auntie and cousins are going to live there for three years. <u>When it got dark, nobody moved and we carried on chatting until midnight</u> because we all knew that they wouldn't be here next year.

Reading and Use of English

Part 1

Vocabulary – Words often confused

1 Look at the Exam tip together. Ask students to do A–D in 1 and then discuss their answers. If they are struggling to see the difference, get them to look the expressions up in their dictionaries and write down some more examples. They could also work in pairs, each pair writing a sentence with one of the expressions. Some of them can then be read aloud and the class can judge whether they have got the right meaning. The best ones could be written on the board as further examples.

Now ask students to do 2, check the answers and ask them what is different about this question. Question 1 tests just meaning whereas Question 2 is dependent on grammar – *depend* and *believe* can be followed by a preposition, *demand* can't be followed by a pronoun (we don't say *He demands us*), whereas *expect* can (*He expects us …*).

When practising for Reading and Use of English Part 1, to help students remember some common expressions like the ones with *at*, you can get them to use their dictionaries to write down several examples in different contexts.

See the Workbook for further practice on words often confused.

Answers

1 A at least   B at once   C at last   D at all
2 A expects   B demands   C depends   D believes

2 Ask students to skim the text very quickly without worrying about the missing words and tell them not to look at the questions 1–8. Tell them you are going to time them – one minute. This is a useful skill for Reading and Use of English, and Listening. Check their answers to the questions. You could ask a couple of extra questions such as:

What was important to the people in northern countries and why? (the seasons and the weather because they were hunters)

What did they use to share? (meals)

How did they celebrate? (they lit fires and candles and sang and danced)

Answers

1 It is the shortest / longest day.
2 that the days will start to get longer and lighter

Exam task

Students do the task. Remind them to read before and after the gaps.

3 When everyone has finished, tell them to quickly read through the text again to make sure the word they've chosen fits. Sometimes when you read the whole text, you realise something doesn't make sense.

Check the answers and discuss any common mistakes.

Answers

1 B   2 D   3 B   4 D   5 C   6 A   7 B   8 A

CLIL Students could choose a country in the far northern hemisphere and find out more information about how the people celebrate midwinter and midsummer there, both today and in the past. Some suggestions are Sweden, Norway, Denmark, Estonia, Finland, Latvia, Lithuania, Canada (Quebec).

Students could research different festivals around the world. You could have a display of each of the festivals chosen with a description and pictures. These could then be used as practice for Speaking Part 2. Students can compare two festivals – clothes, entertainment, food, etc.

Friends

Speaking

Part 1

1 04 In the first part of the exam, students are asked personal information about themselves. The questions are designed to make the candidates feel at ease and give them time to settle into the exam. However, they will of course be marked on what they say.

Students should make sure they can talk about their own lives – school, family, leisure time, future plans, likes and dislikes, etc.

The questions here are examples of the kind they might be asked in the exam. They start by listening to two students answering the four questions. The notes summarise what they will talk about and students should add anything extra they say.

When they have listened, ask students what kinds of things George and Francesca added to the basic information (they talked about when, where, who with, how often, why, and gave more details). Students should get used to asking themselves these questions when they give an answer – is there anything else they can say about when, where, etc.

Answers

1 every Wednesday after school, favourite time
2 relax first and watch TV
3 Saturdays – friends in city centre, shopping, chatting; Sunday mornings – grandmother
4 Saturday – bus to town with friends as usual, probably cinema; Sunday – practise guitar for concert on Tuesday

---

Recording script

Examiner:	Hello, George. I'm going to ask you some questions about yourself. Do you do any activities after school?
George:	Yes, I do. I'm learning to dive so I have a lesson every Wednesday after school in the pool. That's my favourite time in the whole week.
Examiner:	When do you do your homework?
George:	When I get home from school, I watch TV. I like to relax for an hour so I prefer to do my homework after dinner.
Examiner:	Francesca, what do you usually do at the weekend?
Francesca:	I usually meet my friends in the city centre on Saturdays and we spend all afternoon shopping and chatting. On Sunday mornings, I go to see my grandmother.
Examiner:	What are you going to do next weekend?
Francesca:	On Saturday, I'm going to get the bus to town with my friends as usual and we'll probably go to the cinema. But on Sunday I'll be practising my guitar most of the day as I'm playing in a concert next Tuesday. I know I need to practise a lot before that!

---

2 🎧 `04` Ask students to try to remember what the speakers said and fill in the gaps. Play the recording again for them to check. Go through the answers – these will be used in Exercise 3 to discuss the grammar. Give students the recording script (page 78) so they can underline the answers.

Answers

1 'm learning
2 get; watch
3 'm going to get
4 'll probably go
5 'll be practising
6 'm playing

Grammar – Present and future tenses

3 Using students' answers to Exercise 2, ask the class the questions. Revise the difference between the following: present continuous (George's diving lessons are happening over a period of time) and the present simple (habits); when we use *will*, *going to* and the present continuous for the future; when we use the future continuous.

Refer students to the Grammar reference, SB page 78.

Answers

1 present continuous (*I'm learning*)
2 present simple (*get home, watch TV*)
3 *going to* (intention), *will* (uncertain future plan)
4 future continuous as it's over a period of time
5 present continuous (definite plan)

4 Elicit from students that the sentences in A are correct because these are all state verbs which cannot be used in a continuous tense. Ask them to think of other verbs which behave like this – see Grammar reference, SB page 78, for examples.

5 This exercise practises present and future tenses and state verbs. Check students know that conjunctions like *when*, *after*, *until*, *before*, *as soon as* are followed by the present tense even when there is a future meaning, e.g. *I'm going to do my homework before my friend gets here.*

You could follow up this section by checking students' knowledge of prepositions and determiners with days and times. Write some sentences from the listening on the board with gaps, e.g.:

I have a lesson .... Wednesday (every)
What do you usually do .... the weekend? (at)
I usually meet my friends in the city centre .... Saturdays (on)
.... Sunday mornings I go to see my grandmother. (On)
What are you going to do .... next weekend? (-)

Ask students when we use *on* (before days of the week and dates), *at* (before times e.g. *six o'clock*, *lunchtime*, *the weekend*, *the end of the day*, etc.), no preposition (before *today*, *tomorrow* (*morning*), *this/next* (*weekend*)), *in* (before months, seasons, years).

Answers

1 're meeting
2 want
3 normally spend
4 're going
5 think
6 get
7 'm going
8 go
9 'm writing; 'm going to miss
10 're coming

See the Workbook for extra practice on prepositions and determiners with days and times.

Exam task

Get students to spend a few minutes thinking about what they do after school, when they do their homework, what they do at weekends and their plans. They should make some brief notes of extra information they can give.

Students work in pairs, asking and answering the questions in Exercise 1. Remind them to think about *why, when, who with*, etc.

When they have finished, ask them to think of anything they could do to improve their answers. Discuss any problems with the whole class.

Part 2

6 Ask students to decide which of the words they could use to talk about the first two photographs.

> **Suggested answers**
>
> energetic   concentrate   countryside   exercise   indoors
> outdoors   a quiet spot   fresh air

7 Students work in pairs to think of advantages of spending time in these ways. Discuss as a class and list the advantages on the board.

> **Suggested answers**
>
> Photo 1: they're in the fresh air, having fun together, spend less money
> Photo 2: getting more exercise, more energetic

8 🎧 **05** Play the recording. Students note down the advantages Francesca gives. If you wish, give students the script on page 78 so they can underline the advantages Francesca mentions. They can then compare them to the list on the board.

> **Recording script**
>
> Francesca: In both of the photographs the people are exercising but I think the people in the first photograph are probably much happier than the people in the second one. They're riding their bikes in the countryside whereas the people in the second photo are indoors on the running machines in the gym, which isn't as enjoyable as <u>being in the fresh air</u>. Also, in the gym they are doing things separately instead of <u>having fun together</u>. On the other hand, they are probably <u>getting more exercise</u> as they are being <u>more energetic</u> than the people in the first photograph. In the first photograph there is a group of friends or maybe cousins even and they're excited about going somewhere together. They're probably chatting as well. <u>They'll spend less money</u> than going to the gym as cycling is free.

Grammar – Comparisons

9 Ask students to do the exercise and use it to check that they know how to form comparatives. This is very useful for Speaking Part 2 where they always have to compare and contrast two photographs.

> **Answers**
>
> 1 The people in the first photo are probably much happier than the people in the second one.
> 2 They will spend less money than going to the gym.
> 3 The people in the second photo are indoors, which isn't as enjoyable as being in the fresh air.
> 4 They are probably getting more exercise.
> 5 They are being more energetic than the people in the first photograph.

Refer students to Grammar reference, SB page 78.

> See the Workbook for further practice on comparisons.

10 Students work in pairs to build up a bank of words and expressions that they could use to talk about the other two photos.

Exam task

Students work in pairs, choosing two of the photos each (it is best if they don't compare the same two that were used in the recording). Ask them to think for a minute about what they will say and suggest they can look up some vocabulary if they need to. Make sure they know they need to describe the advantages as well as comparing the photographs. Tell them they are each going to talk for a minute. If everybody starts together you can time them for a minute each.

When everybody has finished, you could ask a couple of students to talk about their two photographs to the whole class.

In the exam, when one student has finished talking about two photographs, the other one will be asked a question connected to the topic. Get students to ask each other, in their pairs, the extra question or ask around the class.

Reading and Use of English

Part 5

1 Ask the class to look at the picture and discuss the questions.

2 Tell students they are going to skim the text very quickly to get an idea of what it is about. They should look for the answers to the questions. Time them for two minutes.

> **Answers**
> 1 Sierra's brother is going on a trip and has asked her to go too. She is very excited.
> 2 Amy feels annoyed that Sierra is going on another trip when she doesn't go anywhere.
> 3 The trip they are all going on.

Exam task

Ask students to read the text again more carefully and answer questions 1–4 as they read. They should underline the words which give the answer to each question. Each question has a tip to help them. When they have finished, they should compare their answers with the students sitting near them. If they think they have made a mistake, they should go back and have another look.

Go through the answers, talking about the tips. For each question, ask students which words gave the key and why they chose it. Make sure you explain the following:

Question 1	Tell students that the questions are always in the same order as the text so when they have found the answer to question 1 then they can look at the next question.
Question 2	One question usually tests a word or phrase whose meaning can be found from the context.
Question 3	Students should always make sure they are reading the right part of the text. There will be something in the question or a line number to direct them to the right paragraph.
Question 4	There is usually a reference question and this often requires reading several sentences or a whole paragraph to find the answer.

> **Answers**
> 1 B   2 A   3 D   4 B

Vocabulary – Matching expressions with similar meanings

3 Ask students first of all to look at the picture and guess what is happening. Then ask them to read the text. Check they have understood by asking:

How has Marcus's attitude towards Jake changed?
How do the two boys react when Jake talks to them?
What does Marcus decide to do?

Ask students to work in pairs to find the parts of the text which match the expressions 1–7. When they are ready, read the text aloud and ask the students to stop you when you come to the part of the text which matches each expression. If time is short, you could ask pairs of students to look for one expression only. Explain that this is a very useful skill because sometimes one word in a question may mean the same as a whole line in the text.

If appropriate, you could follow this up with a discussion about whether Marcus did the right thing.

> **Answers**
> 1 keen to get his approval
> 2 (He) really thought he was better than the rest of them
> 3 very unsure and worried
> 4 relaxed, glad that it wasn't him who had been chosen
> 5 rather annoyed
> 6 suddenly made up his mind
> 7 tackle

Writing

Part 1: Essay

1, 2, 3 Tell students they are going to think about Writing Part 1, the compulsory essay task. Ask them to do the introductory exercise individually first, then discuss their answers with a partner. Questions 1 and 2 ask them to describe their own situation regarding family and friends.

There are no correct answers to question 3, although many students will answer A to the first three questions, and B to the remaining three. You can ask students to raise their hands to show whether they would choose family or friends as the answer to each question. Remember to ask them whether what they say relates to all ages, or only a particular stage in their lives. Get students to agree and disagree with opinions expressed, and give reasons for their choices. Elicit what answers they would give for themselves as teenagers. Make sure they have a few phrases to do this (*In my opinion …; I think that … ; For me …; I agree / don't agree with that because …*)

4 Give pairs two or three minutes to discuss the True/False statements. Go over the answers as a class.

> **Answers**
> 1 F (You have no choice. There is one essay task and you have to do it. It's compulsory.)
> 2 F (You have to write between 140 and 190 words. 190 is the maximum.)
> 3 T (It gives you the topic.)
> 4 T (Family and friends)
> 5 T (Yes, you are asked to give a general opinion, although you can give examples from your own life and experience as well.)
> 6 T (Yes, it should be a fresh idea.)

5 Make sure that students understand that point 3 'your own idea' means simply another idea, different from points 1

and 2. In exercise 3, the ideas of *'takes care of you / gives you advice / teaches you'* overlap with the idea of giving support (point 2) so could be included with that point, but not used as a separate point.

The idea of *'spend most time with'* is given as the first point, so *'have most fun with / get on best with'* would be ideas to use as 'your own idea'.

Elicit other possible ideas from the class for the third point e.g. family often stays the same throughout your life, good friends may be as close as family, some teenagers may not have much family so depend on friends, etc.

6 Ask two students to read the essays aloud, then ask all students to complete the chart with the help of a partner.

Answers

Which is more important to teenagers?	Essay A	Essay B
Main points		
1 time	*friends*	*friends*
2 support	*family*	*both*
3 ?	*teenagers get on better with friends*	*family is there throughout your life, friends change*
Conclusion	*friends*	*family*

Go through the chart, then ask students which essay is closer to their own idea. Make it clear that there is no correct answer, and that you can express whatever opinion you like in the points, as long as they are relevant. You can also draw whatever conclusion you like. Explain that your conclusion could be that family and friends are equally important to teenagers; the important thing is that you write about three points and express a clear view.

The essay should always be written in a formal style. Essay B is slightly less formal than essay A because it contains some short forms and takes a more personal approach. It is still formal enough to be acceptable, and answers the question clearly.

If there is time, you could have a brief class discussion about family and friends, and which is more important to the students personally.

7 Go through the answers with students. There is a follow up exercise in the Workbook.

Answers

Essay A: In addition, they play sport; Yet all teenagers still rely heavily; In general though, I would say; Therefore, I personally think
Essay B: overall I spend slightly more time; As for support; Yet my best friend also helps me; In contrast, some of the friends you make; For that reason, I think that

1 in general   2 As for   3 In fact   4 For that reason   5 Yet
6 In contrast

8 Look at the exam task with the students. Point out that essay tasks will not always be in the same format. The first task was in the form of a direct question, while this one

gives you a statement, and you have to say whether you agree or disagree with it, and give reasons for your opinion. There are always two points given, and you have to think of the third and reach a conclusion.

Ask the students to plan their essays individually, and then to discuss the ideas in pairs. If they find it difficult to think of a third point, you can brainstorm ideas on the board, e.g. (agreeing with the statement) grandparents/older people sometimes have more time to talk than parents; they may be able to teach practical skills like cooking or making things; they have a different view of the world, so you hear different opinions; (disagreeing with the statement) their ideas/experience are out of date/not relevant; they think modern attitudes/fashions are wrong; they have little in common with young people

Set the essay task as homework. Discuss timing. They have to answer two questions in 80 minutes, so should spend 40 minutes on each. If they allow five minutes for planning each question, and five minutes for checking what they have written, this means they should try to write their essay in 30 minutes. As they already have a plan, it's a good idea for them to time themselves and give themselves 30 minutes maximum when they do their homework, then spend five minutes checking their work.

Model answer

Older people can certainly tell us a lot about the past and how the world has changed during their lifetimes. My father's great aunt is 97; she has memories of a time when there were few opportunities for girls, and has lived through wars and political crises that I have only read about in history books.
However, many people also say that older people are out of touch with the modern world of technology. I really don't think it's possible to generalise about this. For example, my own grandparents are still at work and they use computers every day. They send me text messages, and my grandmother has a Facebook page which she uses to catch up with friends and family.
In addition, I would like to say that I have learnt a huge amount about people and feelings from my grandparents. They have a lot of experience and they are very wise. If I have a problem, I talk to them about it, and the advice they give me is usually good.
Therefore, I would like to say that I agree very strongly that we can learn a huge amount from grandparents and older people.

See the Writing Extra in the Workbook for more exercises on writing essays.

2 Exploring the world

Unit objectives

FIRST FOR SCHOOLS TOPICS	travel, places
GRAMMAR	past tenses, prepositions of time, adverb formation
VOCABULARY	cities, towns and villages, adjective suffixes
READING AND USE OF ENGLISH	Part 2: identifying part of speech needed
	Part 3: changing nouns and verbs into adjectives
	Part 6: checking references in gapped sentences
WRITING	Part 2 story: prompts, past tenses, collocations
LISTENING	Part 1: underlining words which give the answer
SPEAKING	Part 3: discussing preferences, agreeing and disagreeing
	Part 4: talking about where you live

Adventure and travel

Reading and Use of English

Part 6

1 As an introduction, students discuss the photos, their own experiences and whether teenagers are attracted to dangerous activities. They are going to read a text about a boy who went on a potentially dangerous expedition to the North Pole, so you could extend the discussion by asking students if they would consider doing things like this, e.g. climbing mountains, sailing around the world alone.

2 The titles of reading texts often help to give an idea of what the text will be about.

> **Answers**
> The title tells you he tried to get to the North Pole but he didn't succeed.

3 Even though Part 6 has missing sentences, it is still worth skimming the text to get a general idea. Check the answers to the questions with the class to make sure they have understood what they read.

> **Answers**
> 1 180 km
> 2 a guide called Doug
> 3 windy and cold
> 4 gaps in the ice were too wide for them to cross

4 This text is shorter than a normal exam task but it gives good practice in the skills required to decide which sentence fits in each gap. Give students time to do the task and check their answers. Discuss any wrong answers after they have done Exercise 5.

> **Answers**
> 1B 2A 3D 4C 5F 6E

5 Students should make sure their answers link forwards and backwards. Read through the Exam tip with the class. Point out that this exercise looks at pronouns and the adverb *there*. Look at any wrong answers and establish why they don't fit in the gap. Ask the class the following questions:

Why doesn't A fit in 1? (because no distance is mentioned and 'previously' doesn't refer to anything).

Why doesn't E fit in 3? (there is nothing in the text before the gap which makes sense with 'as bad as').

> **Answers**
> 1 'there' in A refers to the North Pole / his destination
> 2 'them' in B refers to the few people who had skied to the North Pole
> 3 'they' in C refers to temperatures
> 4 'him' and 'his' in D refer to Doug
> 5 'that' in E refers to gaps in the ice
> 6 'these' in F refers to cracks

Exam task

Point out to students that the Exam task has one sentence removed from each paragraph as in the exam (but there are only four gapped sentences here instead of six). There is also one sentence which doesn't fit anywhere as in the exam.

> **Answers**
> 1E 2A 3B 4D

6 When students have checked their answers, ask them to look at any mistakes they made and decide why they were wrong. They should then underline words in the answers which help them fill the gaps. Discuss why C doesn't fit ('they were not the only ones' and 'that' don't fit anywhere). You could also ask the following questions, pointing out that the sentences after the gap are often just as important as those that come before:

In A, what does 'those details' refer to? (there aren't any bears in the Amazon or tigers in the Sahara)

In B, who are 'they'? (the first sea *explorers*)

In D, what does 'that last attempt' refer to? (cycling down the steepest hill and 'that' is also picked up in the sentence which follows)

In E, what do 'most of it' and 'the main theme' refer to? ('most of it' – the book about adventurers and explorers; 'the main theme' – the reference to doing things no one else had done is after the gap)

Answers

A Of course, at some point I realised that I'd got some of <u>those details</u> muddled.
B <u>They knew they could be killed</u> at any moment through their lack of knowledge or poor judgement.
C doesn't fit anywhere
D <u>That last attempt</u> ended in disaster, for the only thing I achieved was broken bones.
E <u>Most of it</u> went over my head, but <u>the main theme stayed</u> with me.

Grammar – Past tenses

7 Ask students to go back to the text 'My future as an explorer' and underline an example of each of the following: present perfect, past simple, *used to*, past continuous. Go over the answers with the class:

> present perfect: *'ve always wanted* (ask students why the writer doesn't say *I wanted* – the writer suggests they still want to be an explorer so uses the present perfect)
>
> past simple: *was, asked, wanted, knew*
>
> used to: *used to lie, used to think* (ask about *used to* – something the writer often did in the past but doesn't do now)
>
> past continuous: *was sleeping* (ask students why this tense is used – to show the activity continued over a period of time in the past).

Students then complete the exercise which practises the difference between the past simple and past perfect. They could compare their answers in pairs.

When they have checked their answers, ask the following questions to check they understand the difference between the past simple and the past perfect:

Look at the verbs about what Parker did on the trip. Which tense are these in?
Which verbs are in the past perfect? What are those sentences about?

Refer students to the Grammar reference, SB page 79.

Answers

1 attempted 2 had reached 3 had travelled 4 went
5 had been 6 were 7 hadn't / had not seen 8 flew

> See the Workbook and CD ROM for further practice on *for / since / ago* with past tenses. There is also practice in the Writing extra section of the Workbook.

CLIL Students could research a young person who has broken a record or attempted to do so, e.g. sailors Laura Dekker, Jessica Watson, Mike Perham, Zac Sunderland, Abby Sunderland, mountaineers George Atkinson, Jordan Romero, Arjun Vajpai, Leanna Shuttleworth.

Reading and Use of English
Part 2
Grammar – Tenses and prepositions

1 Prepositions are often tested in Part 2. Ask students to do the exercise and then check their answers. They can use the Grammar reference SB, page 79 if they need help with the tenses. Ask what the difference between *during* and *for* is (*during* is used for when something happened – *during the night/summer*, etc.; *for* is used to say how long – *for three weeks/two hours*, etc.)

Answers

 1 bought
 2 until
 3 looked; was happening
 4 during
 5 've been trying; haven't finished
 6 was coming; saw
 7 at
 8 'd forgotten
 9 for
10 had disappeared

2 Look at the illustration together. If students know anything about the Bermuda Triangle, talk about what the text might be about. Alternatively, students could be asked to find some information about the Bermuda Triangle before the lesson, and write a short paragraph about it. Students should skim the text for understanding before they do the task but at the same time they can practise deciding what kind of word fits in each gap (in this Exam task they are mostly parts of verbs or prepositions but there will be more variety in the exam).

Answers

Prepositions: 0, 3, 4, 5
Parts of a verb: 1, 2, 6, 8
(7 is a pronoun)

Exam task

Students do the task and compare their answers. When you have checked the answers, point out that 1 tests a fixed phrase as well as the verb tense and 3 tests a phrasal verb. Both fixed phrases and phrasal verbs are commonly tested in this part.

Answers

1 taken 2 was 3 across 4 At 5 until 6 had 7 none
8 have

CLIL Students could do a history project on the Bermuda Triangle. Groups of students could look at different things that happened and then they could have a debate or discussion on some of the theories.

Part 3

Vocabulary – Word building (1)

3   These are quite common adjective endings.

> **Answers**
> -ABLE: bearable, considerable, desirable, fashionable, forgettable, predictable, reliable, remarkable, suitable
> -AL: accidental, central, controversial, cultural, logical, natural, universal
> -OUS: adventurous, furious, mysterious

4   Suggest that students make a list of words they have problems spelling so they can revise them regularly.

> **Answers**
> Nouns and verbs ending in -y usually change the -y to an -i (*reliable*, *furious*, *mysterious*).
> Nouns and verbs ending in -e usually drop the -e (*desirable*, *central*, *cultural*, *natural*, *universal*).

Exam task

Ask students to read the text through first to see what it is about. Remind them that the title will help them. Ask them which part of speech they need for each gap (1, 2, 3, 7 and 8 adjectives; 4, 5 and 6 nouns). Remind them also of the information in the Exam tip.

> **Answers**
> 1 adventurous   2 exciting   3 cultural   4 choice   5 locations
> 6 photographer   7 natural   8 unforgettable

> See the Workbook for practice on the suffixes: -*ism*, -*ship*, -*ness* with nouns; and -*able*, -*ish*, -*ful* and -*less* with adjectives.

Where you live

Speaking

Part 3

1   As preparation for the Speaking task, students think about their own experiences.

2   They compare their lists in groups and explain their choices by using some of the expressions.

3   They can talk about these questions in their groups and then come together as a class to compare their answers.

4   Students work in threes. They categorise the expressions which they should then try to use in the Exam task. Direct them to the Exam tip.

> **Answers**
> A
> I agree with you.
> That's what I think too.
> I think you're right.
> D
> I don't think that's a good idea.
> I think it would be better to. ...
> I disagree.

Exam task

Tell the students that there are always two things they should do – they should talk about each of the suggestions in relation to the situation (whether the places would be popular with teenagers) and then try to come to a decision (which two places they think should be built).

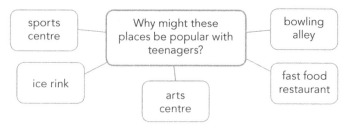

Part 4

5   Students tick the words and expressions they could use. Tell them they can add any others they can think of.

6   In pairs they answer the questions.

Exam task

Brainstorm some possible opinions if you think your students will struggle to come up with them. Then ask them to work in pairs. Tell them they should ask their partner 'why?' if they don't give a reason for their opinions. Have a round-up of what everybody said when they have finished.

Listening

Part 1

1   Ask students to think about what it would be like living in the three cities and how they are different. They are:
A Sydney   B London   C Venice.

Have a brief class discussion about how different these places are from where the students are living now.

2   🎧 **06** Play the recording and check the answer.

Play the recording again and this time ask students to write down the words which helped them match the speaker with the picture. Talk about any useful vocabulary in the other two pictures.

> **Answers**
> Picture C (Venice) – bridges over the canals, pedestrian side streets, beautiful buildings, museums, flooding

> **Recording script**
>
> *Speaker 1*
> Yeah well, I've lived here all my life, and I think that makes me really lucky! There's water all around you and bridges over the canals and lots of little pedestrian side streets. And then there are lots of beautiful buildings, palaces and churches – some of them are museums now. It's very flat everywhere though, so we get flooding.

3 🎧 07 Play the recording of an example of a Part 1 and check the key.

Answers
C

Recording script

Girl: Well, it's my hometown and I love it! People eat out quite a lot here and you'll find everything from Brazilian food to Spanish tapas. But if I go out with my family, we usually eat Italian: pasta and pizza. What I find absolute magic about the city though is the street celebrations – they take place all year. In winter, when the snow falls and the days get shorter, we have the Lights Festival in the main square, which is really fantastic. And then of course there's the underground city which is basically a huge shopping mall. I often go there with my sister – she just adores it, but I find it a bit too big!

4 🎧 07 Play it again and, if possible, give the students a photocopy of the text (page 78) or write it on the board.

They underline the words which give them the answer (What I find absolute magic = what she particularly likes; the street celebrations = the outdoor festivals).

Ask why A and B are wrong.

A is wrong because the shopping mall is what the girl's sister likes; she thinks it's too big.

B is wrong because the girl simply says she eats out, not that she particularly likes it.

Exam task

🎧 08 Give students a minute or two to read through the questions. Tell them the question always tells them who is talking and what about. It also asks them something specific so it's really important they read carefully before they listen. Play the recording twice.

Answers
1 A   2 C   3 B   4 C

Recording script

You will hear people talking in four different situations. For questions 1–4, choose the best answer A, B or C.

1 You hear a boy talking to his aunt about his new school.

Woman: So, Peter, are you happy at your new secondary school?

Peter: Yeah, very. I've made lots of new friends. It's good because we work well together in class, too, everyone does, there's no messing about … although we are occasionally the students that get told off for chatting too much!

Woman: Right …

Peter: … and it's great learning a language. I'm doing Chinese this year. We've got a lovely teacher, who's really enthusiastic about her subject.

Woman: Sounds good.

Peter: And it's a modern building, with a sports field and a cafeteria. There's a big courtyard too, where you can sit outside and relax between lessons. There was nowhere like that at my last school …

2 You hear two teenagers talking about a film they have just seen.

Girl: So, what did you think then?

Boy: Great, really exciting … I loved the car chases and all that stuff where he was leaping over the roofs. Much better than too much talking …

Girl: But the characters were really good. What they said was quite funny at times. You like fast-moving films then, do you, with a bit of adventure?

Boy: Yeah, doesn't everyone?

Girl: Well, not everyone. I do though. That and some nice scenery to look at – loved the mountains in this one.

Boy: Oh, didn't notice. Liked the film though.

3 You hear a girl talking about a school trip she has been on.

Girl: Yeah, well, we went on a cool trip last week to a modern art gallery. It was in a fantastic building with amazing architecture. It used to be an old factory, and there was just, like, so much space everywhere. There was a sort of library with lots of books and film clips, and it was just so comfortable, with all these big cushions you could sit on. I found out a lot about the background of the person who designed the stuff in the special exhibition on textiles. They were beautiful to look at … really rich colours. I'd love to know what inspired the shapes and patterns on them.

4 You hear two teenagers talking about a friend.

Boy: Hi, Lauren. Have you seen Mike recently?

Lauren: Yeah, his leg's still in plaster. Such a shame he broke it just before the big match. He's in good spirits though, not being miserable, even though he missed his big chance. I think that's fantastic. It was such a shame he couldn't take part in the final though.

Boy: I know. He's one of their regular players, so I bet the football team missed him. I'm pleased he's reacted okay.

Lauren: Yeah … he'll be able to play again in a few months. That must be encouraging for his team-mates.

Boy: I suppose so. Let's hope they get some goals tomorrow.

Lauren: Right, we can always hope …

Writing

Part 2: Story

1 Students look at the pictures and discuss in pairs the order they should go in. When they have decided, check the order:

Answers
The order is: 1 E   2 B   3 D   4 A   5 C

2 Look at the exam task together. Explain to the class that the story task in the exam paper is given a context (e.g. writing something for a school magazine or a competition). You are then given the first sentence of the story, and two other elements to include.

Students work in pairs. They should look at the vocabulary in the box, and say which pictures the words are in. Then they should try to tell the story verbally. Ask one pair to tell their version to the class and see if the others agree with it.

Grammar – Past tenses

3 Students can work through the story and choose the correct verbs on their own, then compare answers with their partner. Check answers with the class.

> **Answers**
> 1 looking (the participle belongs with *I was* and describes a continuous action over a period of time)
> 2 knew (the verb *know* is not used in the continuous form)
> 3 had (past perfect because you are thinking of a period of previous time, before this story starts)
> 4 had built (as 3)
> 5 heard
> 6 realised (the verb *realise* is not used in the continuous form)
> 7 was
> 8 called
> 9 've (present perfect for a very recent action in the past; the plate is probably still in his hand)
> 10 rushed
> 11 was going (continuous action over a period of time)
> 12 disappeared
> 13 didn't
> 14 got out (one action)
> 15 shone (one action)
> 16 'd
> 17 had

4 Students read through the story again and divide it into three paragraphs, and then say what each part is about. Correct by eliciting answers from class.

Explain that it is a good idea to divide a story into at least three paragraphs, possibly corresponding to setting the scene, main events and what happened as a result/in the end. However, open-ended stories, that ask a question or leave an unanswered mystery, are also acceptable in the exam.

> **Answers**
> Paragraph 1 ends after 'centuries ago', and sets the scene for the story.
> Paragraph 2 ends after 'disappeared down into a deep hole' and describes the main events of the story.
> Paragraph 3 describes what happened to the writer and what he found.

5 Look back at the exam task in exercise 2. Ask them if the story in exercise 3 follows the instructions (it does). It is important to follow the instructions exactly to get a good mark. Their stories should be 140–190 words in length.

Ask students to look at stories A and B, and with a partner work out a story that follows from the prompt sentence and includes the two elements underneath. They should

also decide how the story will end. Give them ten minutes preparation time, then compare two or three versions of each story.

Students can write one of these stories for homework, timing themselves (5 minutes planning, 30 minutes to write, 5 minutes to check).

Vocabulary – Adverbs and adjectives

6 Point out to students that this exercise tests useful collocations that they can use in their stories. Read the information in the Exam tip with the class.

> **Answers**
> 1 a worrying 2 a courageous 3 an intriguing 4 a strong
> 5 a successful 6 aggressive 7 a brilliant 8 a detailed

> See the Workbook for further practice on *-ing* and *-ed* adjectives.

7 Ask students to work in pairs to choose the correct answer. After the exercise has been completed, ask students to write sentences in which the wrong answer is used correctly. Check answers round the class.

> **Answers**
> 1 calmly 2 positively 3 decisively 4 rapidly 5 efficiently
> 6 patiently 7 closely 8 regularly

Grammar – Adverb formation

8 Students work in pairs to complete the exercise.

> **Answers**
> 1 bitter 2 clumsy 3 happy 4 hopeful 5 miserable
> 6 positive 7 polite 8 rapid 9 rare 10 simple
>
> 1 Adjectives ending in *-y* change their last letter to *-i* before adding *-ly*: clumsy, happy
> 2 Adjectives ending in a consonant and *-le* lose the last letter before adding *-y*: miserable, simple
> 3 Adjectives ending in *-e* keep the *-e* and add *-ly*: positive, polite, rare
> 4 Adjectives ending in *-l* keep the *-l* and add *-ly*: hopeful

Exam task

Look through the bullet points together.

Model answer A

Max heard someone calling his name excitedly, and turned to see who it was. It was his friend Peter who rushed over saying that he'd won a prize, a trip to America. 'And there are four tickets,' he said. 'My Mum and Dad are going. Do you want to come with us?'

Max didn't hesitate to say yes. And that was how he found himself on a flight to Florida. At the airport, they picked up a hire car and Peter's dad drove them to the hotel. Max and Peter ran rapidly to the swimming pool where they spent a couple of hours swimming and diving.

Then they headed off to the theme park, where they ate hamburgers and tried all the rides, including one very scary rollercoaster, which made them both scream when it reached full speed. And then, right at the highest point, it suddenly stopped. All the electricity had gone off. It was very hot sitting in the sun, but there was nothing they could do except wait patiently until a successful rescue attempt was made. Fortunately, nothing else went wrong during the rest of the holiday!

190 words

Model answer B

I was amazed when I saw who was sitting in the seat opposite mine. I'd just sat down on the train and I couldn't believe it was him at first. Then when he looked up and smiled warmly at me, I knew I was right. What was the most famous football player in the world doing on this train, sitting calmly, reading a football magazine?

I thought I'd ask him. 'Excuse me, David. Why are you travelling by train?'

'Well,' he said, 'I'm supposed to set a good example to everyone, and not throw my money around, because I do a lot of charity work with young people. Actually I quite like travelling by train. If anyone talks to me, they're usually very polite, like you are. And I like chatting to people.'

That was the best news I had heard in a long time. I asked my hero lots of questions about his work, his family, and when he first discovered he had a talent for football. He answered them all patiently, and before we arrived in London he gave me a signed photo of himself as a souvenir.

190 words

 CLIL

Students can research famous archaeological finds on the Internet and write a paragraph about what they found out for homework (e.g. Tutankhamon, Sutton Hoo, Chinese Terracotta warriors).

3 The entertainment industry

Unit objectives

FIRST FOR SCHOOLS TOPICS	entertainment
GRAMMAR	passive, linkers
VOCABULARY	film and cinema, music
READING AND USE OF ENGLISH	Part 4: sentences with the same meaning
	Part 7: matching information in question and text
WRITING	Part 2 review: making a plan, describing and recommending
LISTENING	Part 4: predicting what you will hear
SPEAKING	Part 1: adding comment and opinion
	Part 2: avoiding words you don't know, giving preferences

Films

Listening

Part 4

1 Before the students open their books, elicit from them the names of jobs in the film industry and put them on the board. Then ask students to work in pairs to complete the box with the words and phrases connected to making a film. Let them use a dictionary to find out the meaning of unknown words if necessary. Check the answers before moving on to the next exercise.

Answers

Person	What (s)he does
actor	acts, performs, plays a part/role
stuntman/woman	does action shots
set decorator	arranges the scenery
director	tells the actors what to do
cameraman/woman	films a scene, takes a shot of something
producer	raises money to make the film
costume designer	designs/fits costumes
sound technician	checks quality of voice recording
make-up artist	does someone's face/hair

See the CD ROM for more vocabulary practice.

2 Ask students to describe the people in the photos and say what they are doing. Check answers with several different pairs so the whole class has heard the responses.

Suggested answers

Picture A: A cameraman is filming a scene on set. There are young actors who are getting ready to film a scene. The woman on the left is the director. She is telling the actors what to do.
Picture B: A make-up artist is doing someone's face and hair.
Picture C: A costume designer is about to fit a costume.
Picture D: A stuntman is doing an action shot in a film.

3 Ask students to underline two or three important words in the instructions and in each question. This is a useful skill to practise as it helps them to focus on the important points of the Exam task. The first question is done as an example. Check underlining with the class, getting a different person to suggest the underlining in each question.

Suggested answers

You will hear part of an interview with a young actor called Tania West.

2 In what way is Tania like Angie, the character she plays in the film?
   A She doesn't get on well with other people.
   B She doesn't try to impress other people.
   C She doesn't always behave as other people expect.

3 What did Tania find difficult about being on set?
   A working with older actors
   B learning her lines
   C having little time to relax

4 What does Tanya say about her acting schedule?
   A She often filmed at night.
   B She had little trouble getting up early.
   C She missed having regular meals.

4 Point out that the instructions and questions to a Part 4 listening give a lot of information about what they will hear. Ask students to predict, in pairs, what will be in the recording, and tick the topics Tania will talk about.

Suggested answers

a problem she has had
her reactions to her own acting
her own personality
her daily routine

Exam task

🎧 09 Point out that there are usually seven questions in the Exam task, although in this task there are only four. Do the task as in the exam, listening to the recording twice. Check answers. Read through the Exam tip as a reminder.

Answers
1 B   2 C   3 C   4 B

Recording script

You will hear part of an interview with a young actor called Tania West. For questions 1–4, choose the best answer A, B or C.

Interviewer:	So Tania, welcome to the studio.
Tania:	Thank you, it's great to be here.

Interviewer:	Tania, you've just finished your first film and been to the opening night – and you're still only 17! What was it like seeing yourself on screen?
Tania:	Well, it was kind of weird at first. It's like looking at a giant version of yourself. Before I went to the opening I thought it might be scary, but it wasn't in the end. I just felt like I was watching my twin! <u>Somehow it just wasn't me up there</u>, yet I could remember how many times I'd had to do the scene, how much of me had gone into it. I certainly wasn't bored watching the film, even though I knew it so well. Everything suddenly came to life …
Interviewer:	And were there any similarities between you and Angie, the girl you played on screen?
Tania:	Yeah, well it would be nice to think so! <u>She's a bit of a rebel, and I'm a lot like that. I often don't follow normal rules.</u> She doesn't really care what people think about her though, whereas I do. But because she's very confident, people find it easy to relate to her. I did anyway. I found myself just walking round the studio, pretending to be Angie. That's how I really got into the role. I missed her when we finished shooting!
Interviewer:	What was the atmosphere like when you were on set? Did you have any problems?
Tania:	Actually, I found it quite stressful. <u>We were on a tight schedule, and there was never any time just to chill out.</u> You were always learning your lines, but fortunately I found that easy because I've got a good memory and the older actors helped me. You form a close bond with other actors, they kind of become like your family really. They were a big part of my life for several months.
Interviewer:	And how did you find the daily schedule at the studio? Did you get into a routine?
Tania:	We had to be on set, have our make-up done and everything by 7.30, <u>so that meant getting up very early. Fortunately, my family lives quite close to the studio and it didn't bother me.</u> All the actors had breakfast together, and then we shot some scenes, maybe three or four each morning. Then everyone ate lunch and then we shot more scenes in the afternoon. Then on a few occasions, we did night-shoots too, and that didn't finish till about two a.m. …
Interviewer:	But you enjoyed it?
Tania:	Oh, yes!

CLIL Students can discuss in pairs or small groups which job in the film industry they would like to do and why, and what would be good and bad about doing the job.

Writing

Part 2: Review

1 Before students open their books, elicit the names of the different types of film they know and come up with a list like the one in question 1. Then ask them what makes a film enjoyable, and elicit the words in question 2. Ask students to open their books and do questions 1 and 2 in pairs. There are no right answers, but you can compare answers in the class as a whole.

2 Ask students to look at the photos and discuss the questions in pairs.

> **Answers**
> The photos are of: Indiana Jones, James Bond, Batman, Lara Croft. Other answers will be personal, although the class could vote on their favourite hero/heroine.

3 Ask the students to read the Exam task and then answer questions 1 and 2 in pairs. Check as a class.

> **Answers**
> 1 You can write about **any** type of film, provided it features an impressive hero/heroine. The word *hero* could be used for a man or a woman.
> 2 The question asks you whether you would **recommend** the film, so it's possible to write a negative review if you think that the storyline or other actors are not good. But the hero you write about must be impressive, and it's much easier to write about a film you enjoyed!

4 Tell students to read the exam candidate's review and answer the four questions in pairs. Then check answers together.

> **Answers**
> 1 Yes, especially the hero and the villain.
> 2 Yes, because it says the film makes you think and that it's interesting.
> 3 Present tense. The alternative is the past tense. Either is acceptable, but you must be consistent about your use of tenses. Write the whole review either in the present tense, OR in the past tense(s), but don't use a mixture of the two.
> 4 The candidate gives the work a title so the reader knows immediately which film is being talked about.
> 5 The sentence which sums up the candidate's view of the film is: *In my opinion, this film is outstanding*.

5 Ask students to underline the words and phrases used to describe the film, Batman and the Joker and put them under the correct heading. They should also say whether they are positive or negative.

> **Answers**
> **film:** dark N; difficult N; disturbing N; amazing action scenes P; outstanding P; thrilling P
> **Batman:** action hero P; symbol of justice P; brave P; determined P
> **Joker:** psychopathic N; scary N

6 Tell students it is important always to write a plan before they write and ask them to complete the one for a review of *Batman: The Dark Knight*. Ask them to check answers with a partner before discussing the answers with the whole class.

> **Answers**
> **Para 1** introduction – describe film, makes you *think* + amazing action scenes
> **Para 2** content of film – describe Batman and his *character* and how he fights organised *crime* and *The Joker*
> **Para 3** conclusion – sum up film and *recommend* it (explain why)

7 Ask students to underline any linking words or phrases in the review that they could use to write their own review. If possible, show the review on the whiteboard and get students to come to the front to underline their suggested answers.

Answers

This is a classic in the Batman series. It is a dark, difficult and at times rather disturbing film <u>which</u> really makes you think. <u>As</u> you sit in the audience you wonder what would happen if a hero like Batman really came along and decided to deal with organised crime in our big cities, <u>yet</u> you are <u>also</u> entertained <u>because</u> the film has a lot of amazing action scenes.

In *The Dark Knight*, Batman is an action hero, <u>but more importantly</u> he is <u>also</u> a symbol of justice. He is a brave and determined character <u>who</u> teams up with the forces of law and order in the city of Gotham, ready to take on all the crime lords. <u>As a result,</u> he has to face a psychopathic and very scary villain called The Joker.

<u>In my opinion,</u> this film is outstanding. It is <u>not only</u> thrilling <u>but</u> it <u>also</u> makes you feel as if you are experiencing what is going on. <u>When</u> I saw it, everyone in the audience was totally involved in it, <u>so</u> I'd say it's a film you really must see.

8 Ask students to do the exercise in pairs, naming the film they would review in exercise 1, page 23. You could have a class vote for the best film ever, or the favourite film in several different genres.

Exam task

Ask students to choose one of the tasks and do it either in class, or for homework. Draw their attention to the bullet points after the Exam tasks.

Model answers

The best thriller ever: Bullitt

I saw this old film again recently on DVD and it's still fantastic. It stars Robert Vaughan as an ambitious politician who wants to fight organised crime and Steve McQueen as Bullitt, one of the detectives whose job is to protect him. The film has a very complicated plot. Bullitt has to be very clever to catch the criminals and stop the politician from being murdered.

The film is still famous after many years because it has some amazing action scenes, with Bullitt driving a green Ford Mustang car. The most famous scene is a car chase, with two bad guys chasing Bullitt up the hills in San Francisco. They go everywhere, including up and down the steps that San Francisco is famous for. It's so exciting it takes your breath away! The other great chase is at the airport, on the runways. It's amazing.

I would definitely recommend this film. In my opinion, it is outstanding. It makes you feel as if you are experiencing what is going on. You will enjoy it because the action scenes keep you on the edge of your seat.
182 words

Romantic Comedy: One Day

This is a very interesting story because of the way it is told. The two main characters, Dexter and Emma, meet at university and become best friends. They both get romantically involved with other people, and there are lots of amusing moments. The film explains how their lives turn out by showing you what happens over the years on just one day each year.

There are big highs and lows in this film. At first you think Dexter and Emma will never get together, but in the end they do, and for a while they are incredibly happy. But then the film changes; it all ends in tragedy, and Dexter is nearly destroyed as a person, until his father is able to rescue him and show him how to get on with his life and make a new start.

I really liked it; the ending is very unusual for a romantic comedy. It's not what you expect at all which I think is one of the best things about the film. I'd recommend anyone who enjoys romantic comedies to see this film.
182 words

 As an extra task you could point out to the class that reviews can be of many different things. Students could use the Internet to find some examples and make a list of the things reviewed.

> **NB** Candidates will not be asked to write reviews of specialist products of which they have little experience. The topics candidates might be asked to write about include TV programmes, websites, books, music and shops.

> See the Workbook for further vocabulary practice. There are some exercises on writing reviews in the Writing Extra in the Workbook.

Music

Reading and Use of English

Part 7

1 Have a class discussion about the kinds of music students like, including any that aren't listed. You could do a quick class survey of the most popular bands, singers, etc.

Then check students know the names of all the instruments in the picture and get them to work in small groups to decide which instruments would be in a rock band, a jazz band and a classical orchestra. They can add any other instruments they know. You may want to discuss which instruments students play and if anyone plays in a band or orchestra.

Answers

The instruments are (left to right): guitar, flute, drums, clarinet, violin, saxophone, keyboard, cello, piano

Most commonly the guitar, drums and keyboard are in a rock band and a jazz band which could also have the clarinet and saxophone. The classical orchestra is more likely to have the flute, the violin, the cello and the piano.

2 This provides practice in the skills needed for Part 7 – reading for detail and checking that the words in the question match what the text says. Get students to work individually and then check their answers with a partner. Ask them to underline the words in the text which match those in the questions.

Answers

1 ✓ (contains songs = <u>have lyrics</u>, whose words will appeal to a certain age group = <u>which focus on the kinds of emotions that teenagers really relate to</u>)
2 ✗ (the text says the opposite – <u>there's no way you could describe it as depressing</u>)
3 ✗ (<u>it seems things can only get better for them</u> so it will probably be more rather than less popular than the last one)
4 ✗ (the last album <u>introduced a new sound</u> which this one develops)
5 ✓ (likely to extend the success = <u>expected to further widen the band's appeal</u>)
6 ✓ (particular style = <u>a very unusual voice</u>, well matched = <u>they suit him perfectly</u>)
7 ✗ (the writer is happy with most of the singing being <u>done by Kez</u>)

3 Time the students while they quickly read through the texts and answer the three general questions. Have a brief discussion about their answers. The reviews are mainly positive.

Exam task

Ask students to do the Exam task individually and then compare with their partners. Check the answers and discuss any wrong answers. The texts will be longer in the exam and there will be ten questions. There are often only four texts as here but there can be up to six.

Answers

1 D (will set high standards for her second)
2 B (some tunes are difficult to distinguish from each other)
3 A (focusing on topics other artists seem to prefer not to sing about)
4 C (her teen audience is sure to mature and grow along with her)
5 D (there are several songs that could easily have been left out, resulting in a better album overall)
6 A (after a two-year wait, in spite of pressure from fans and their record company)
7 B (the best song is not the most well known)
8 C (While some bands ... the Lantanas are by contrast a rare find)

Grammar – Linking words

4 Ask students to find the relevant sentences (paragraph letters are given in the answers below). Then, either look at the Grammar reference, SB page 80, together or elicit the difference between the linkers by writing more example sentences on the board.

Ask students which of the linkers have the same meaning (*in spite of* and *despite*; *even though* and *although*).

This exercise highlights common mistakes with these linkers.

Answers

A Breeze has released *Pedal Street* after a two-year wait, <u>in spite of</u> pressure from fans and their record company to do so earlier.
B <u>However,</u> she then shows just what the band is about with the roaring, angry growl that follows. <u>Although</u> some tunes are difficult to distinguish from each other in the sense that Tarrant's voice doesn't vary from song to song, the album will soon be permanently fixed on your playlist.
C <u>While</u> some bands incorporate good beats but have cliché lyrics that make you feel slightly sick, or sing songs with meaningful words, yet make a dreadful sound, the Lantanas are by contrast a rare find.
D <u>Despite</u> having a more limited vocal range than her sister who is also a singer, April proves that she does have a big talent for writing.
It is an excellent combination of easy listening <u>even though</u> there are several songs that could have easily been left out, resulting in a better album overall.

Answers

1 Despite / In spite of   2 However,   3 even though / although
4 Even though / Although   5 However,   6 Despite / In spite of

---

See the Workbook and CD ROM for further grammar and vocabulary practice.

Speaking

Part 1

1 This exercise is designed to encourage students to say as much as they can in the first part of the Speaking test. The example shows them a useful exam technique for doing this, which they then practise in the exercise. Students should first do the exercise alone.

2 Students practise asking questions and giving the answers in pairs, making sure they add extra information and an additional comment or opinion.

Part 2

3 Students often find it difficult to think of ideas to talk about, so looking at the pictures and writing a list of things they can say is a useful exercise. Point out that in the exam the questions at the top of the page are designed to help them think of things to say and they should make sure they answer them.

4 🎧 [10] Ask students to listen to the recording and put a tick next to any of the things they hear which are the same as the ones on their list. Compare answers around the class.

5 🎧 [10] Get the students to listen again, and ask them to complete the missing words in the sentences. These phrases will help them to express themselves when they need a word they don't know.

> **Answers**
>
> 1 ... you know the sort of films which have drawings not actors
> 2 ... these people are ... well, let's say a bank has just been robbed or something like that
> 3 It's a special kind of street dance I don't know the name of ...
> 4 ... the children in the photo of the school orchestra they look very ... well ... er ... um ... I'd say definitely not relaxed.

Recording script

Examiner:	In this part of the test, I'm going to give each of you two pictures. I'd like you to talk about the pictures on your own for about a minute, and also to answer a question about your partner's pictures. *[to candidate A]* It's your turn first. Here are your pictures. They show people watching different kinds of films. I'd like you to compare the pictures, and say what you think people might enjoy about these films. All right?
Candidate A:	Well, in the first picture, a mouse is being chased by a cat and I suppose he'll be caught soon. When I was a child, I used to like programmes like this very much, <u>you know, the sort of films</u> which have drawings not actors. I think children always like them, and adults often enjoy them, too.
	In my opinion, the film in the second picture is more exciting. It's a thriller and these people are ... <u>well, let's say</u> a bank has just been robbed <u>or something like that</u>. That's why the men in the black car are being chased by the police. They'll probably be arrested soon and will be taken to the police station. Most young people like thrillers, especially if there is a lot of action and a nice hero or heroine. People of all ages like them actually.
Examiner:	*[to candidate B]* And which of these films would you prefer to see?
Candidate B:	OK, I'd prefer to see the second film. I'd definitely enjoy the thriller. I think it's better to see a really exciting film that you can enjoy and get involved in.
Examiner:	Thank you. Now, here are your photographs. They show people playing music in different situations. I'd like you to compare the photographs, and say why you think music is important to these different groups of people.
Candidate B:	Well the first photo shows some kids dancing to music in the street. It's a special kind of street dance <u>I don't know the name of</u>. The music is being played on a sound system with huge speakers. Most of the people are smiling and they look happy. I guess this is just their way of escaping and having fun. It's all part of their image too, part of their identity. And then when you look at the other picture, the children in the photo of the school orchestra ... they look very ... <u>well ... er ... um ... I'd say</u> definitely not relaxed. They look like this is something they have to do. I guess some of them were persuaded to do it by their parents or a teacher. I think they might be rehearsing for a concert and I expect the concert will be attended by the parents. I suppose it will prove to them that their children are very talented, so maybe it's a big challenge for them ... for the children I mean ...
Examiner:	Thank you. *[to candidate A]* And which of the activities would you prefer to do?
Candidate A:	Mmm ... that's a difficult choice because I'd sooner not do them at all.
Examiner:	Why not?
Candidate A:	I can't dance very well, and I'm not the slightest bit musical! But perhaps if I had to do one of them, I'd rather play in the orchestra than do dancing in the street ...
Examiner:	Thank you.

---

6 In pairs, get students to say which four words they think the candidates didn't know, then underline the words they used to hesitate in the sentences above. Words used to hesitate are underlined above in the recording script.

> **Answers**
>
> cartoons   robbers   breakdance   serious / stressed

7 🎧 [11] Play the last part of each candidate's turn which is recorded separately. Students tick the phrases used to make a choice or express preferences as they hear them (all are used). Then ask students to practise asking the questions above the pictures and answer with the phrases given.

> **Answers**
>
> The candidate uses *I'd prefer to ..., I'd definitely* and *I think it's better to ...* to answer *Which of the films would you prefer to see?* The candidate uses *I'd sooner ...* and *I'd rather ... than ...* to answer *Which of the activities would you prefer to do?*

Recording script

Examiner:	And which of these films would you prefer to see?
Candidate B:	OK, I'd prefer to see the second film. I'd definitely enjoy the thriller. I think it's better to see a really exciting film that you can enjoy and get involved in.
Examiner:	Thank you.

Candidate A:	Mmm ... that's a difficult choice because I'd sooner not do them at all.
Examiner:	Why not?
Candidate A:	I can't dance very well, and I'm not the slightest bit musical! But perhaps if I had to do one of them, I'd rather play in the orchestra than do dancing in the street ...
Examiner:	Thank you.

Exam task

One student asks the question above one pair of pictures. The other talks for one minute using the skills they have learned in the unit (hesitating, avoiding unknown words, expressing choice and preference). They then change roles and the other student practises with the other two pictures.

Reading and Use of English

Part 4

Grammar – The passive

1 🎧 **10** Play the recording again so they can check their answers. Students complete the sentences with the correct form of the passive. Correct the sentences as a class.

> **Answers**
> Candidate A
> 1 A mouse <u>is being chased</u> by a cat and I suppose <u>he'll be</u> <u>caught</u> soon.
> 2 ... a bank <u>has just been robbed</u> or something like that. That's why the men in the black car <u>are being chased</u> by the police. They'll <u>probably be arrested</u> soon and <u>will be taken</u> to the police station.
>
> Candidate B
> 3 The music <u>is being played</u> on a sound system with huge speakers.
> 4 I guess some of them <u>were persuaded</u> to do it by their parents or teacher.
> 5 ... I expect the concert <u>will be attended</u> by the parents.

2 Put the table on the board, and get the students to complete it with verbs from the listening (not in italics below. Passives from reading text and questions are in italics.)

tenses	verb form	past participle
present simple	are	felt
present continuous	is / are being	chased / played
future simple	will be	caught / arrested / taken / attended / fixed
past simple	was/were	persuaded / recorded
present perfect	has been	robbed / allowed / looked forward to
past perfect	had been	told
with modals	could have been would be	left out improved

3 Ask students to look back at the reading texts and questions on page 26 and find eight more examples of the passive to add to the table. Elicit the remaining tenses if you wish. Refer students to the Grammar reference, SB page 80.

> **Answers**
> (Passives from reading text are in italics in chart.)
> Fans <u>had been told</u> to expect something special (A)
> Emotions that <u>are felt</u> by everybody (A)
> which <u>was recorded</u> over two years. (B)
> the album <u>will soon be permanently fixed</u> on your playlist. (B)
> <u>Lena has been allowed</u> to sing all types of song here. (C)
> <u>could</u> easily <u>have</u> <u>been left out</u> (D)
> <u>would be improved</u> (Q5)
> <u>has been looked forward to</u> for some time (Q6)

4 Ask students to correct the mistakes in the sentences individually. They then discuss in pairs.

> **Answers**
> 1 This castle **was built** in the twelfth century.
> 2 I was give**n** a leaflet which contained some interesting information.
> 3 The band **was** first established in 1992.
> 4 These days music **is made** by computers.
> 5 My best friend **is** called Ann-Marie.
> 6 The concert **was** supposed to start at 7.00, but the guitarist arrived late.
> 7 My house **is** located in a beautiful area.
> 8 The business studies course **was** cancelled at the last minute.
> 9 **Is** lunch include**d** / Will lunch **be** included in the price of the school trip?
> 10 My family stay in a house that **is** situated a few miles from the beach.

5 Go over the instructions for Reading and Use of English Part 4. Emphasise that you can only use between three and five words in the gap. Ask them to do examples 1–5 in pairs, choosing the correct answer and saying why the other answers are wrong. Correct together.

> **Answers**
> 1 A is correct. B is in the wrong tense; C is grammatically correct but doesn't use the prompt word *been*.
> 2 B is correct. A *disappointed* is wrong; a noun is needed. C has too many words and doesn't use the prompt word 'was'.
> 3 C is correct. A is in the wrong tense; B is missing the verb *be*.
> 4 A is correct. B is missing the verb *is*; C has the wrong preposition *to*.
> 5 C is correct. A and B both include *to* and B also omits ''d*.

Exam task

Ask students to do the sentences on their own. Point out they may have to make more than one change in the sentence, and not just put the verb into the passive. Get them to compare answers with a partner before checking answers as a class.

> **Answers**
> 1 was built by
> 2 was knocked over by
> 3 has been played more
> 4 will have been handed in
> 5 will be worn by
> 6 will be given less

> See the Workbook and CD ROM for further practice of the passive and *have something done*.

4 Active life

Unit objectives

FIRST FOR SCHOOLS TOPICS	sports, health and fitness
GRAMMAR	modal verbs, prepositions following verbs and adjectives
VOCABULARY	sports, food
READING AND USE OF ENGLISH	Part 2: choosing the right preposition
	Part 3: nouns ending in -ence, -ity, -ion
	Part 5: finding the right part of the text
WRITING	Part 2 letter and email: giving advice and making suggestions
LISTENING	Part 2: deciding what part of speech to listen for
SPEAKING	Part 3: asking opinions and reacting
	Part 4: expressing an opinion

Sports

Reading and Use of English

Part 5

1 Ask students to work in groups and guess which the most popular sports are worldwide and in their own country. Compare answers around the class and talk about why these sports are the most popular.

> **Answers**
>
> The top five sports in the world are football, cricket, hockey, tennis and volleyball.

2 Ask students to do the exercise and compare the answers. There are some general rules which might help them to remember. Ask students if they can see any pattern but point out there are lots of exceptions (*play* is often used with ball games, *go* with sports ending in *-ing*, *do* with sports that are often done as an individual rather than as a team game). Ask students to add any other sports they are interested in.

> **Answers**
>
> do athletics   play badminton   play cricket   go cycling
> play football   do gymnastics   play hockey   go ice skating
> do martial arts   go snowboarding   go surfing   play tennis
> play volleyball   go windsurfing   do yoga

> See the Workbook for an exercise on common expressions with *make* and *do*.

3 Students discuss the questions in pairs and compare answers around the room (these are common questions in the Speaking test).

4 Go through the words together and ask students to tell you the answers.

> **Answers**
>
> *Football*: defender, goalkeeper, net, opponent, penalty, pitch, referee, tackle
> *Tennis*: court, net, opponent, point, serve, umpire
> *lap, race* and *track* are used for athletics (or track and field) and motor racing.

5 When students quickly skim a text to find out what it is about, it is a good idea for them to try and think about the main point of each paragraph. This stops them focusing on the details at that stage.

> **Answers**
>
> A – Paragraph 3
> B – Paragraph 4
> C – Paragraph 2
> D – Paragraph 1

Exam task

The questions in this part usually relate to one paragraph each, although some paragraphs may contain the answer to two questions. Get students to read the first paragraph and answer question 1, check the answer and then let them go on to the second paragraph and second question, etc.

> **Answers**
>
> 1 D   2 C   3 A   4 B

> See the Workbook and CD ROM for further vocabulary practice.

Listening

Part 2

1 For this part of the test students should always read the questions before they listen and think about what kind of word is needed in each gap. Ask which gap needs an adjective and then ask what kind of word is needed in the other gaps (nouns).

> **Answers**
>
> Sentence 4 needs an adjective.

2 Although students have established that 1, 2 and 3 need a noun, only some of the words will fit the sense.

> **Answers**
>
> 1 brother, friend, photographer, sister, uncle
> 2 friend, photographer, post, rock, tree
> 3 brakes, route, tyres, weather
> 4 comfortable, stylish, tight, warm

3 🎧 `12` Students choose the answers from the words in the list. Point out that the other words are often used as distraction, e.g. in question 1 *brothers, friends, sister* and *uncle* are all mentioned. Play the recording twice.

Answers

1 uncle   2 photographer   3 tyres   4 tight

Recording script

Freya: When I was about 13, my dad bought my brothers a mountain bike each because all their friends had one but, because we were girls, my sister and I were given ordinary bikes that were no good for racing. I really wanted to join my brothers, so in the end my <u>uncle</u> got one for me and my sister.

My sister never really got into it but I spent all my time out on my bike and started to enter competitions. I just won the Regional Championship and I beat all the boys. It was a difficult course with lots of rocks and stony bits and at one point I thought I wasn't going to win. I was ahead and then I had to slow down because a <u>photographer</u> jumped out from behind a tree.

I am very careful with my preparation for races. I look at the route and make sure everything's working on the bike. The brakes need to be in perfect condition especially if the weather's wet. Then, just before I set off, I take a look at the <u>tyres.</u> If there's any problem with them, then I'll be in trouble. Also, it's really important to wear the right clothes. They shouldn't get in the way or slow you down so they need to be <u>tight.</u> They might feel a bit uncomfortable when you first put them on but you soon get used to it. I'm not bothered about looking fashionable or stylish – I just want to win.

Exam task

🎧 `13` Give students time to read the questions. Ask them to think about the kinds of words which might fit in the gaps. They could make some guesses. Play the recording twice. You could then give students a photocopied script (page 79) so they can check their answers.

Answers

1 second (Ask them who came in third – his brother)
2 stretch (Ask why he stretches and why this is the most important thing – it keeps him flexible and free from injury)
3 audience (Ask why he doesn't think about the judges – he makes mistakes)
4 S/stars on ice (Ask why Ice Champions is wrong – he watched this when he was a child)
5 music (Ask what they can't choose – partners and routine)
6 swimming (Ask why he doesn't go horse riding or play tennis – he can't fit them in)

Recording script

You will hear part of a talk by a young skater called Karl Milton. For questions 1–6, complete the sentences with a word or short phrase.

I'm training very hard at the moment because I'm hoping to be picked for the Olympic ice-skating team. I should have been in the team four years ago – well, that's what my coach said. But I was left out, so I'm determined to be selected this time. I competed in a national championship last week and so did my brother – he skates too. Jack Graham was defending the title – you might have seen him on TV afterwards – and he must have been practising all the time as he was even better than last year and finished first. But I was <u>second</u>, just behind him, and my brother came third so we were both pleased. Either of us could have won but you just never know who's going to do best on the day.

To be good enough to win competitions, I need to be really fit. Obviously I practise every day and I spend a lot of my time on the ice doing spins and jumps to get them exactly right. But I skate really badly if I ever forget to <u>stretch.</u> That's really crucial and something all skaters have to do, so I spend about thirty or forty minutes doing that every day before and after I go on the ice. It keeps me flexible as well as free from injury.

I enjoy competitions but I do get nervous, so I never think about the skaters I'm competing against. I just focus on the <u>audience</u> and hope they're enjoying it – then I skate well. If I start thinking about the judges, then I make mistakes.

And something new for me, I'm going to be a judge myself soon. I always loved the TV show *Ice Champions* when I was a child and now I'm going to be one of the judges of *Stars on Ice,* which is for teenagers. I'd say to any contestant wanting to do well, you should build up your confidence so that you put on a really smooth and entertaining show. Each skater has a partner. They can't choose who they skate with and they have to follow a certain routine, but they can decide which <u>music</u> they want to skate to.

I'm hoping one day to have more time for hobbies. I go <u>swimming</u> whenever I can – that was my first love before skating and it helps me with my moves on the ice. I'd love to go horse riding or play tennis, but although they would be good for building up muscles and fitness, I can't fit everything in! And now I need to go and do some training …

Grammar – Modal verbs

4 Students try to complete the gaps from memory. If necessary, play the recording again.

Check the answers and explain any wrong answers (there are explanations in the Grammar reference, SB page 81).

> **Answers**
> 1 should   2 can't   3 have to   4 can   5 should have been
> 6 must have been practising   7 could have won

5 This checks students' understanding of the modals which they have heard in context.

> **Answers**
> is allowed – 4 (can)
> seems certain – 6 (must have)
> is advised – 1 (should)
> isn't allowed – 2 (can't)
> was possible – 7 (could have)
> is a rule – 3 (have to)
> was expected – 5 (should have)

6 Ask students if they know the difference between *must* and *have to*, *mustn't* and *don't have to*. Write some examples from the Grammar reference (page 81) on the board to help. Students can use the Grammar reference if they need it to help them do the exercise.

> **Answers**
> 1 don't have to   2 should   3 must have been   4 mustn't
> 5 had to   6 must

> See the Workbook and CD ROM for further practice of modals.

Speaking

Part 3

1 Ask the class which activity they would use to get fit and which to have fun. Students could then work in pairs, each pair taking one activity. They should think about the questions in the bullet points and write some notes of what they might say. Go through each idea as a class.

2 Point out the difference between two people taking turns to talk and actually having a conversation. If you're having a conversation, there are links between what the people say. Go through the expressions that can be used to keep a conversation flowing.

Exam task

Then look at the Exam task together – there is always a particular context (talking about sport at school, etc.). Check they have noticed the two things they have to do – talk about whether all students have to do sport at school and how often they should do sport at school each week. Ask students to work in pairs to talk about the activities. They should use the conversation techniques.

Time them for two minutes. When two minutes are up, check whether students had enough/too much time and what they should do to fit the discussion into two minutes. Now tell them they have one minute to decide which two

activities they would choose. When they have finished, see which two activities were the most popular choices.

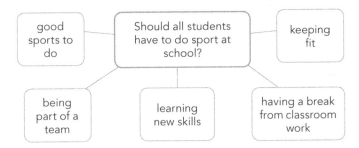

Part 4

3 Read the question together and give students time to read the opinions. See how many people agree with each one.

4 Discuss any other opinions the class might have on the topic.

Exam task

Students work in pairs to discuss the other questions.

Keeping fit and healthy

Reading and Use of English

Part 2

Grammar – Prepositions following verbs and adjectives

1 These expressions are all commonly tested in this part. They have been chosen from the Cambridge Learner Corpus from those that students often make mistakes with.

> **Answers**
> 1 on   2 for   3 of   4 with   5 about   6 of   7 about   8 about
> 9 in   10 to

> See the Workbook for more practice of other similar expressions.

Exam task

Point out to students that this part mostly tests grammar and fixed expressions. Remember to point out the Exam tip. Ask them to do the task individually. They should always read the whole text through when they have finished to check it makes sense. They can then compare their answers in pairs. Go through the answers.

> **Answers**
> 1 the   2 or   3 in   4 on   5 there   6 your   7 such   8 like

> See the Workbook for an exercise on *it* and *there* (Q. 5 in the Exam task) and an exercise on common phrases for Reading and Use of English Part 2.

Part 3

Vocabulary – Word building (2)

2 Do this together. Point out that these are quite common suffixes that are often tested.

> **Answers**
> similarity (similar +ity)
> conclusion (conclude ~~de~~ +sion)
> suggestion (suggest +ion)

3 Students work in pairs to make nouns. Check their answers. Point out that in the exam they have more help as the words are in a context.

Ask them to look at the nouns they have written. Which ones just add the suffix to the word (like *connect / connection, equal / equality, react / reaction*). What happens to adjectives ending in *-t* (like *confident / confidence, convenient / convenience, independent / independence, patient / patience*). Most words lose one or two letters before they add the suffix. Some words have a spelling change, e.g. *curious / curiosity, generous / generosity, possible / possibility*.

> **Answers**
> confidence   convenience   curiosity   equality   generosity
> independence   patience   possibility
> appreciation   concentration   connection   decoration
> division   expansion   production   reaction

> See the CD ROM for an exercise on noun suffixes.

Exam task

Tell students to quickly read through the text. Check they have understood it by asking them:

What is the text about? (the history of fast food) *Why were the first fast food restaurants opened?* (cars became more popular) *What is happening to fast food now?* (It's getting healthier.)

Ask students to look at each gap and check what kind of word is needed (they are all nouns except 3 and 8 which are adjectives and 4 which is an adverb). Get them to do the task individually and then check the answers.

> **Answers**
> 1 popularity   2 madness   3 successful   4 increasingly
> 5 variety   6 introduction   7 choice   8 unacceptable

Vocabulary – Food

4 Talk about what kinds of foods are healthy and whether students think they have a healthy diet. Ask students to make adjectives from the nouns. (When a noun ends in a vowel and one consonant (e.g. *nut*), we often double the consonant when we add a suffix; *salt* ends in two consonants so we don't double the *t*.)

> **Answers**
> fatty   nutty   salty   spicy   tasty

5 Ask them to do the vocabulary exercise and check the answers.

> **Answers**
> *diet*: balanced, healthy, low-fat, rich, vegetarian
> *meat*: fried, low-fat, raw, rotten, tough
> *fruit*: raw, ripe, rotten, seasonal
> *pudding*: rich, sugary

CLIL Students research a traditional meal from different countries. They then come together in groups and compare their meals to decide which is the healthiest.

Writing

Part 2: Letter and email

1 Ask students to read the exam task, then with a partner discuss what advice they would give Alex. Elicit one example of each of the structures you want them to use on the board first, e.g.

I'd advise / recommend him to play tennis.
I'd suggest / recommend taking up athletics.
He could / should do volleyball.

Get feedback from the class as a whole about which sport Alex should do and why. You can take a vote.

2 Ask students to read the reply, and then to put the phrases into the correct gap in the letter, looking very carefully at the structures before and after the gap.

> **Answers**
> 1 don't worry too much about   2 remember that   3 it should
> 4 it'd be better to   5 I suggest you   6 Why not
> 7 recommend doing   8 you can

3 Ask the students to read the letter again, and answer the questions in pairs.

> **Answers**
> 1 T   2 F (He talks about all three.)   3 F   4 T
> 5 F (He wishes him luck.)   6 T (The style is fairly informal i.e. it's
> direct, and Pete uses short forms, but the letter doesn't contain
> lots of slang or idioms; it's grammatically correct.)

4 Point out that the layout of the letter and email is different, but that the technique for writing the reply is basically the same.

Ask students to read Annie's email and then in pairs to suggest some activities for her, using the phrases in exercise 1. Get some suggestions from the class as a whole. e.g. *I suggest going cycling. I'd recommend spending time in the mountains. She should take up an outdoor sport like hockey.*

5 Ask the students to read Susie's reply, and put the correct sentence into each gap. They should check their answers in pairs, and then discuss whether the email is better with or without the extra sentences. The email reads better with the extra sentences because there is more detail and interest. The writer is adding personal opinion and experience, and improving the way the email flows.

> **Answers**
> 1 E   2 C   3 A   4 D   5 B

6 This paragraph gives advice about answering the email/letter question on the Writing Part 2. Ask the students to do the task in pairs.

> **Answers**
>
> 1 informal 2 friend 3 will 4 don't 5 usually (there will sometimes be a request for information about something e.g. … so please send me some information about what happens in your country.) 6 both are acceptable 7 should 8 less than (and it's better to write 170–190)

7 Students discuss the answers.

> **Answers**
>
> All can be ticked except 'Yours' and 'With kind regards'.
> **Start:** *Hi* and *hello* are more informal, and often used in emails. *Dear* is often used in a letter.
> **Finish:** *All the best, best wishes, Good luck with everything, Love, Hope that helps* are good ways of finishing informal letters and emails. *Yours* and *With kind regards* are found at the end of formal letters and emails.

Exam task

Get students to discuss what advice they would give to Sarah and Sam, so they have ideas for their own writing. Students can then write their own reply to the letter or email in class, or as homework. Encourage them to use the structures from the unit and the phrases they have learnt in the lesson, and to read the bullet points carefully before they write. They can also time themselves (5 minutes planning, 30 minutes writing, 5 minutes checking time).

> **Model answers**
>
> A
> Hi Sarah
> Well, I think going to spend two weeks with your German pen friend sounds like a wonderful idea. I wonder why your parents don't want you to go? If it's very expensive to get there, then I can understand why it's a problem. Otherwise, I'm sure you will be very safe staying with a family, you'll learn about everyday life in Germany and you'll certainly come home speaking the language better.
> So, what can you do to persuade your parents to let you go? Well, perhaps you could ask your German teacher if she would speak to them about it as I'm sure he or she will think it's a good idea. Or ask your pen friend to ask her parents to write to your parents. That way they will know it will be a good educational experience for you, and that you will be comfortable with the German family. My only other idea is that you ask your pen friend to stay with you first, so your parents will know that she is a nice girl of the same age.
> Does that help? Write and let me know, won't you?
> Love
> Anya x

> B
> Hello Sam
> It sounds as though you are in a difficult situation. I know you've always loved football, and I know you are also a good drum player, so it's a tough choice. But actually, I wonder if you have to choose?
> There will probably be football matches every week, but I'm sure you will only have concerts once or twice a term and you'll know in advance when they are going to be. If that's right, why don't you explain the situation to your football coach, and ask if it's okay if you miss a match occasionally? There are always other players who can take your place, aren't there, so perhaps he will be okay with the idea? If that's no good, then you'll have to make a choice. You know I'd always choose the sport; it keeps you fit, and you make lots of friends in the team. And as you know, I'm not at all musical. But for you, I don't know – maybe just do whichever will make you happier. And if everything else fails, toss a coin!!
> Good luck with it.
> All the best
> Pieter

> See the Writing Extra in the Workbook for more exercises on writing emails and letters.

5 Learning

Unit objectives

FIRST FOR SCHOOLS TOPICS	achievement, ambition and education
GRAMMAR	conditionals, *unless, in case, as/so long as, provided/providing (that)*
VOCABULARY	education, careers, phrasal verbs
READING AND USE OF ENGLISH	Part 1: choosing the correct phrasal verb
	Part 4: conditional structures
	Part 7: the difference between words with similar meanings
WRITING	Part 2 set text: contents and question types
LISTENING	Part 2: listening for the cues before the gaps
SPEAKING	Part 1: giving explanations
	Part 2: making guesses and giving reasons

Ambitions and achievements

Reading and Use of English

Part 7

1 In this part, it is important that students make sure the question says exactly the same as the text in the answer they choose. There will usually be another text which says something similar but not exactly the same. Get students to match the words and meanings in pairs, using a dictionary if they need to. The words are all B2 in the English Vocabulary Profile. When you have checked the answers, ask students what the other words mean.

> **Answers**
>
> 1 sympathetic   2 communicative   3 adventurous
> 4 competitive   5 creative   6 capable

2 Check students know what the jobs are in the photographs.

> **Answers**
>
> A climbing instructor   B nurse   C (infant) teacher   D sculptor

3 Get students to work in pairs or small groups and decide what qualities are important for the jobs. If they can, they should add more adjectives.

> **Suggested answers**
>
> climbing instructor – adventurous, capable, communicative, energetic
> nurse – capable, cheerful, communicative, decisive, sympathetic
> (infant) teacher – capable, cheerful, communicative, creative, energetic, sympathetic
> sculptor – creative, thorough

4 Ask students if they would like to do any of these jobs and say why/why not. Ask them which job they would be most suited for.

Exam task

Look at the Exam tip. This is one way of doing the task. Another way is to read all the texts quickly and then go through the questions in order but this usually takes longer. Give students ten minutes to answer the questions. If they haven't finished, give them another five minutes. They should aim to do each part of the Reading section in less than 15 minutes.

> **Answers**
>
> 1 D   2 B   3 C   4 A   5 B   6 D   7 B   8 C   9 A   10 D

Reading and Use of English

Part 1

Vocabulary – Phrasal verbs

1 Tell students that phrasal verbs are often tested in Part 1 of Reading and Use of English. Ask them to look at the examples, then say what a phrasal verb is. Accept that it's a verb used with a preposition at this stage, but say that some words are a different part of speech, although they look like prepositions (see below).

Get the students to find the verbs in the questions on page 38 and the texts on page 39 and underline them.

2 Ask students to guess the meaning of the words they have underlined, and then match them with the answers. Check answers together.

When they have done this, you may want to talk about phrasal verbs and how they are used. Alternatively, you can talk about them before using the exercises in the Workbook for this unit.

Sometimes the meaning of a phrasal verb is clear (*The sun came up over the mountain.*) and sometimes it is idiomatic, so the verb doesn't have its usual meaning (*He went off cheese.*).

On other occasions the same phrasal verb can have different meanings.

Put these sentences with *give in* on the board and ask students to tell you what the phrasal verb means in each.

I gave in my homework on time. (= give to someone else for checking or reading)

Jack knew he couldn't win the game but he wouldn't give in. (= accept defeat)

A phrasal verb consists of a verb and a preposition or an adverb. They look the same, but the word order used with them varies according to whether the verb is followed by an adverb or a preposition. Some phrasal verbs have both a preposition and an adverb, e.g. *get on* (adverb) *with* (preposition).

Put the examples of phrasal verbs below on the board and put a tick or a cross next to them when you have told students the rule.

When a phrasal verb consists of a verb and a preposition, they can't be separated:

He went off magic. ✓ (*He went magic off.* ✗);

He came across an old photograph. ✓ (*He came an old photograph across.* ✗)

Three part phrasal verbs like *come up with* cannot be separated.

When a phrasal verb consists of a verb and an adverb, they can be separated and they don't always have an object:

He gave up, He gave up magic or *He gave magic up* are all correct.

The best way to check whether a phrasal verb consists of a verb + preposition or adverb is to use a dictionary. If students aren't sure what to do, they should simply avoid putting the object between the two parts of the phrasal verb.

Answers
1 come up with 2 put up with 3 come across 4 give up
5 point out 6 look down on 7 look up to 8 stand out

See Workbook Unit 6 for more practice of phrasal verbs.

Exam task

Ask students to read the text quickly to get a general impression of it. Then ask them what the teenager's dream was, and how it came true. Ask students if they have any dreams or ambitions like this for the future and briefly discuss as a class. Students do the task on their own, then check answers in pairs before you go through them as a class.

As a follow up, you could ask students to write an example sentence for each of the phrasal verbs in questions 1, 2 and 5, using a dictionary if necessary. Listen to a few examples to check that word order is correct.

Answers
1 C 2 A 3 B 4 D 5 B 6 C 7 D 8 A

Part 4

Grammar – Conditionals

3 Ask students to complete the sentences in pairs, and then check their answers with the texts on page 39.

Answers
1 'd spend 2 wouldn't have found out 3 'll have to 4 have to

4 For each of a–d write the completed sentences from Exercise 3 on the board. Then get students to tell you which matches which kind of conditional (4: zero, 3: first, 1: second, 2: third). Underline the verbs in each.

Answers
a 2 b 3 c 1 d 4

5 Explain that there are other phrases which are used like conditionals. Get them to read the sentences in pairs and match them with the meanings in 1–3. Check answers.

Answers
1 unless
2 in case
3 providing (that) / provided (that); as / so long as

6 Ask students to choose the correct answer in questions 1–4. Tell them to think about the meaning if they are unsure of the correct answer.

Answers
1 unless 2 if 3 in case 4 so long as

See the Workbook and CD ROM for more practice of conditionals and related phrases.

Exam task

Read the instructions with the students and check they have remembered that the sentences must have the same meaning, they mustn't change the word in capitals and they must use it. A contraction e.g. *isn't*, counts as two words. Get students to do the exercise on their own, then check with a partner before checking together as a class.

The example given is with a phrasal verb; the other sentences except 5 all test conditionals, or related phrases.

Answers
1 unless we practise 2 provided my sister is 3 in case there is not / isn't 4 would have done some 5 looking forward to finding 6 need to practise (for)

Education

Listening

Part 2

1 Write the word 'education' in the middle of the board. Students brainstorm the words connected to education that they know. Elicit them and write them on the board, including as many from Exercise 1 as you can.

Then ask students to open their books, and make sentences about themselves using the words in Exercise 1.

2 🎧 14 Tell students they are going to listen to an English girl called Anna talking about her education. As they listen, they tick the words in Exercise 1 that she uses.

Recording script

Anna: I attended a <u>primary</u> school in the village where I lived. I started when I was four and stayed there until I was 11, when I moved to the secondary school where I am now. Both are state schools, so they're free, and my secondary school is comprehensive, but we're streamed for certain subjects like maths and languages. I'm much better at numbers than words, so I'm in the highest group for <u>maths</u>, but not for languages. I'm in the second set for those and I study Spanish and German. We all go to school in uniform, and put on special sports kit whenever we're playing sport of any kind. For the girls, it's <u>blue shorts</u> and a white polo shirt. They're very practical.

Moving to secondary school was quite hard for me because it meant catching the <u>school bus</u> instead of walking, and the school is very big – there are over 1,000 pupils. The facilities are good though. There are playing fields at the back where we can do sport, and there's a proper canteen. And there are science laboratories and quite a big library and a swimming pool. My life's very busy now. I get homework every night, and I play in the school orchestra and the hockey team.

3 Ask students to look at the four words that Anna uses in the recording and match them with the words underlined in the sentences in Exercise 4 below.

Point out to students that this exercise is showing them a useful strategy for Part 2 of the listening exam. The answers to the questions will usually be introduced by a word which means the same as the one they hear in the recording, but which isn't identical.

Answers

attended – went to   catching – getting   highest group – top set
put on – wear

4 🎧 **14** Play the recording again, and get the students to complete the answers.

Answers

1 primary   2 maths   3 blue shorts   4 school bus

5 Divide the students into small groups and ask them to talk about questions 1–4 together. Check answers as a class, asking one person from a group to give feedback on each question.

CLIL Students could use the Internet to find out whether most countries have comprehensive schools and streaming, and draw up a chart or graph to show their findings.

6 Explain that students are going to think about educational visits. Get them to work in pairs to answer the questions, then check answers quickly as a class.

7 Tell students they will hear a boy talking about an educational visit. Ask them to look at the photos in pairs and think of five words they think they might hear in his talk. Check vocabulary as a class and write it on the board.

Suggested answers

plane, wing, shelter, pilot, cockpit, control, radio

8 Ask students to look at the words underlined in the Exam task questions and match them to the words in the box. Check answers and tell students they will **hear** the words in the box on the recording.

Answers

1 not far from   2 building   3 didn't appear   4 press
5 defended   6 amazed   7 hard   8 described   9 built
10 came to a close

Exam task

🎧 **15** Get students to do the Exam task on their own. Check answers as a class. Play the recording twice.

Answers

1 airport   2 rock   3 maps   4 button   5 attack   6 jets   7 size
8 servicing   9 wood   10 radio

Recording script

You will hear a student called Max talking about his visit to the Aeroseum in Gothenburg, Sweden. For questions 1–10, complete the sentences with a word or short phrase.

Max: Well, I'm going to talk about my visit to the Aeroseum in Gothenburg in Sweden. I went there with my technology class. It was really interesting and we all enjoyed it. We arrived about half past nine in the morning and we were met by our guide, who fortunately spoke very good English!

The museum is located in some underground shelters not far from a former <u>airport,</u> which was used by the military. Building the shelters was a huge project. Work started in the 1940s and then continued in the 1950s. The guide told us that they had to carve out and move tons of <u>rock</u>, which is much harder than digging out earth. And we found out later that no-one knew anything about the existence of the shelters till just over twenty years ago, when work on creating the museum began. That was because they didn't appear on <u>maps</u> and were kept secret, even from people who lived locally.

And when you enter the museum, you realise how much thought went into the design. First you have to press a <u>button</u> outside the main doors. As each person does this the number on the counter screen changes, so you can see exactly how many people are inside at any one time – that's a safety thing. Then there is a loud 'beep' and the doors slide open. They weigh about 180 tons and are about a metre thick, so the building would have been well defended against <u>attack</u>!

I was expecting to see some really old planes, so I was amazed that the first thing you see when you go in are some jets, which look as if they could have been built quite recently. I got a very clear impression of what the shelter was like when it was in active use in the 1950s. And the great thing about this museum is that nothing is off limits; you can climb into any of the exhibits. I really enjoyed getting into one of the cockpits. I was expecting the controls to be complex, but the size of it astonished me. It was so small. It must have been really hard for the pilot to cope with.

After that, our guide told us about the photo gallery, which has pictures of the site construction, and photos of the people who lived and worked in the building over the decades. I didn't find that so interesting, but later on we met a man who volunteers in the gallery now and was happy to describe his experiences of flying planes from the airport and servicing them underground. That was fascinating.

Another thing I really liked was watching people hard at work restoring some of the old planes. The amazing thing was that some of them were working on a wing, and the frame was built of wood, just like the models I've been making. Once that had been made, the wing was covered with fabric, using lots of layers to give it strength. I have to say it didn't look very strong to me, and it was very delicate work!

We stopped for refreshments and then spent more time looking at other aircraft displays before making our way through some of the service tunnels, which were used to bring in supplies, and then going to the control room, where we learned all about 'holding patterns' – the way aircraft are held above the airport, circling round until they can land. We then moved into the radio room, where another volunteer told us about his work and our visit came to a close.

I had a great time. We were there for about three hours and I have to say I could happily have stayed for much longer. I learned a lot and it was really hands on – living history; it meant something to me.

Now, I've got some photos to show you, so if you just hang on …

9 Ask students to check how they did in pairs, and discuss the reason for any wrong answers.

Then draw their attention to the Exam tip. They will hear words which are used to distract. Give/show students a copy of the recording (page 79). Ask them to look for the words which tell them when they will hear the answer to a question. Underline the answer, and put a circle around any other possible but incorrect answers. In the first one, *shelters* is not the answer because it is plural and is already in the sentence, so doesn't make sense.

Point out that sometimes you have to listen to what comes after a key to make sure it fits the gap, e.g. 7 (*size*).

CLIL Students could find information about educational visits in different cities across the world e.g. New York: Ellis Island, London: Globe Theatre, Paris: The Louvre. They could use this information to produce reports for a classroom wall display, with appropriate drawings, photos or pictures.

Speaking

Vocabulary – School subjects

1 Ask students to tick the subjects they are studying at school, then compare with a partner. If appropriate, ask whether they all study the same subjects, or if they can choose which subjects they can study.

2 Ask students to discuss in pairs which of the subjects in Exercise 1 they like best, and explain why. If they have another reason for liking it apart from reasons a–d, they should write it down under *e*. Briefly check a few answers round the class before moving on.

Part 1

3 Ask the students in pairs to match the answers in the speech bubbles with questions 1–4. They should then take it in turns to ask and answer the questions about themselves. Remind them to give extra information whenever they can.

You can also put the following extra questions on the board for students to practise:

Ambitions and achievements

1   Which countries would you really like to visit and why?
2   What have you already achieved?

Education

3   What do you like best about your secondary school?
4   Do you prefer studying on your own or with other people?

Check a few answers around the class before moving onto Part 2.

Answers
1 C   2 B   3 D   4 A

Part 2

4 Tell students that they will work in pairs. One student will be A, the other B. Remind the students that they have to speak for one minute about the photographs.

Go through the phrases they could use to describe the photos if they are unsure of what it is. Then ask student A to compare photos 1 and 2 and say what pupils might learn by doing the different subjects at school (B could time A).

Check that students understand how to use the phrases to explain preference and give reasons, and ask B and A to discuss together which lesson they would prefer to do and why. Remind students that the examiner will ask a question like this in the exam at the end of the task.

Check a few answers around the class.

Exam task

Ask student B to compare photos 3 and 4 and say what they think the pupils will learn on the visits. (A could time B.) When B has finished, ask B and A to discuss which of the visits they would prefer to go on and why.

Writing

Part 2: Set text

You should only do this section if you are studying the current set text as part of the syllabus and think that your students would be able to answer the question well if they selected it in the exam. They will need a firm grasp of what happens in the book and the main characters and events. If candidates write about the wrong book, they will receive no marks for their answer. Set text questions can be in a range of formats i.e. essay, article, letter/email, review. Information about the set text can be found on the Cambridge *http://www.cambridgeenglish.org/exams-and-qualifications/first-for-schools/* Then click on 'Download Information for Candidates'.

Since the set text changes every two years, it is not possible to provide book specific exercises here, but those given can be adapted for use with any book. You will need to do some advance preparation of the exercises yourself before using them in class. It is a good idea to do them after students have read the whole book.

Begin the lesson by telling the students they are going to think about the set text question and ask them to write the name of the book and the author at the top of the page. Explain the importance of answering the question with reference to this particular book (see above).

Techniques for using the exercises in class:

1   Elicit the names of the main characters and put them on the board. In pairs, students discuss how they would describe each of the characters with appropriate adjectives or phrases.

> **Example:**
> Macbeth: evil, under the control of his wife, violent, ambitious, feels very guilty about what he does

When they have finished, brainstorm ideas on the board. Discuss which are the best descriptions of each character and ask students to give reasons for their answer by referring to the book, e.g. ambitious – Macbeth wants to be king of Scotland.

2   Ask students in pairs to write a brief description of what happens in the book. Choose three good answers, and ask students to read them aloud when everyone has finished.

> **Example:**
> *Frankenstein* is about a scientist who decides to create a human being and ends up making a monster. The monster isn't evil to start with, but he looks terrifying, so he can't live with human beings because they are afraid of him. He is lonely, sad and angry, and in the end he commits murder.

3   Ask students in pairs to write a list of what happens in the book they are studying, and to put the ideas in the correct order. They can do this by brainstorming, then looking at the book to check their information. **NB** You will need to prepare a correct version in advance.

> **Example:** *Touching the Void* **Main Events**
> 1 Joe Simpson and Simon Yates decide to climb the west face of Siula Grande, a mountain in the Andes in Peru.
> 2 On the way to the summit, Joe falls and is badly injured.
> 3 Simon tries to get him off the mountain because they are running out of food.
> 4 They both nearly fall off a cliff, and Simon has to make the terrible decision to cut the rope tying them together. Joe falls.
> 5 Simon gets back to base camp, thinking Joe is dead.
> 6 Three days later, he hears a cry in the night. Simon goes out to find Joe alive, despite being seriously injured.
> 7 Both survive and remain friends.

4   You will need to look at the set text questions in advance and prepare a plan for each question before the lesson.

Ask students to look at the questions. Explain that you will read them aloud and complete them with the correct names and the title of the book you are reading together. Explain that the set text question may be an essay, article, letter/email or review. They will **not** have a choice of question in the exam.

5   Divide the class into four groups. Get each group to discuss and plan an answer for one of the questions. When they have finished, one student from each group should present their plan to the class, writing it on the board. Discuss whether this is a good answer to the question.

Exam task

Students write their answer to the question, either in class or as homework. (30 minutes to write, 5 minutes to check)

It is not possible to supply model answers to the questions as set texts change frequently. However, examples of set text answers can be found in the Writing Guide.

> There are more exercises on set texts in the Writing Guide in the SB and the Writing Extra in the Workbook.

6 Natural world

Unit objectives

FIRST FOR SCHOOLS TOPICS	environment, weather, wildlife
GRAMMAR	countable and uncountable nouns, articles, *so* and *such*, *too* and *enough*
VOCABULARY	pollution, climate, animals
READING AND USE OF ENGLISH	Part 2: choosing the correct article for a gap, timing
	Part 6: using linking words to follow an argument
WRITING	Part 2 article: getting the reader's attention, introductions and endings, style
LISTENING	Part 4: ruling out the wrong answers
SPEAKING	Part 3: responding to pictures
	Part 4: talking about the environment

Environment and weather

Listening

Part 4

1 Tell the students they're going to talk about the environment and weather in different countries. Ask them in pairs to look at the photos and identify the words. Let them use dictionaries if they need to.

> **Answers**
>
> A bushes, rocks, sunshine, grass
> B snow and ice, volcano, grey sky, mountains
> C lake, mountains, pine trees, snow and ice
> D grass, sunshine, bushes

2 Ask students to discuss which photo shows which country. Check answers by asking one student which country they thought a picture showed, and then what helped them to decide. Get students to correct each other if necessary.

> **Answers**
>
> A Australia   B Iceland   C Canada   D Cameroon

3 🎧 **16** Tell students they will hear three speakers talking about their country and that they should listen and identify which country they are talking about. Check answers.

Then ask students to listen again and write down some words which gave them the answer. Possible answers are given below.

> **Answers**
>
> Speaker 1 Iceland   Speaker 2 Cameroon   Speaker 3 Canada
>
> 1 volcanoes, island, Arctic, snow and temperatures below zero
> 2 rainy season, very large country, semi-desert, game reserves, giraffes, humid, tropical, rainforest
> 3 cold weather and snow, summer – extreme heat, -25°C, heated houses, the fall

Recording script

Speaker 1

Yeah, well several of the volcanoes in my country have erupted in recent years, and thrown huge clouds of dust into the sky. This ash is dangerous for aircraft, so there have been times when airports all over Europe have had to close down. It's very dark everywhere when a volcano has just erupted. Normally, though, the weather in my country is mild all year because we're an island. Our summers don't get very hot, and our winters are rarely very cold. But because we're located between the cold air and sea of the Arctic and the warmer air and sea of the more temperate countries, we sometimes get several seasons in a day: sunshine and mild temperatures; windy, cool temperatures and rain; snow and temperatures below zero! Weird eh?!

Speaker 2

The cities in my country are getting hotter, and we get a lot of industrial pollution now. In addition, the ocean is warming, and sea levels are rising. We've always had quite a lot of flooding during the rainy season, and that's getting worse, much more extreme. The whole continent is experiencing climate change.

I live in a very large country, so the climate varies according to where you are. For example, in the far north, there's a semi-desert with mineral deposits and fantastic game reserves with giraffes and things. That contrasts with the land along the coast which is humid and tropical, and where there's a mixture of rainforest and farmland. And finally, the areas inland are much cooler and wetter than the coast because there is regular rainfall.

Speaker 3

People often associate my country with cold weather and snow, but in fact the climate is very diverse. There are four very distinct seasons. In summer, temperatures can rise to 35°Celsius and higher, and scientists are saying that this extreme heat will increase with global warming. In winter, when most parts of the country have snow, temperatures fall as low as –25°Celsius but we manage to stay warm because we have heated houses, cars and public transportation systems. Some cities have even installed walkways to and from buildings in schools, although mine hasn't got one yet!

Spring is generally pleasant and very mild. The fall is often cool, but really bright, with rich orange and red leaves on trees. That's certainly my favourite time of year. OK, so …

4 🎧 **16** Ask students to make a list of the adjectives, nouns and expressions the speakers use to describe the weather. Give them a copy of the recording script (page 80). Elicit vocabulary from the class and put it on the board.

> **Answers**
>
> **adjectives:** mild, hot, cold, warm, windy, cool, humid, extreme, tropical, wet, bright
> **nouns:** sunshine, snow, (regular) rain(fall), flooding, heat
> **expressions:** several seasons in a day, distinct seasons, temperatures below zero, the ocean is warming, sea levels are rising, is experiencing climate change, temperatures fall as low as –25°C, rainy season

5 Tell students to tick the words and expressions that can be used about their own country. Then ask them to discuss the weather in their country in pairs. They should then decide what their favourite time of year is and why. Check answers to this around the class.

6 Ask students to identify which of the countries in the box have the problems listed below. They can work in pairs or small groups and use the Internet or books if they need to. Some countries have more than one problem.

Finally, ask students to discuss whether they have any of these problems in their own country and what can be done about them. Get feedback from the class.

> **Suggested answers**
>
> forests disappearing – Brazil
> volcanoes erupting – Italy
> industrial pollution – the USA, Brazil
> rivers drying up – Spain
> lack of rain – Saudi Arabia, Spain
> flooding – the USA, Bangladesh
> hurricanes – Jamaica, the USA
> ice melting – Switzerland

CLIL Ask students to do some research on the Internet and find out which other countries have the problems on the list. The class could then design some posters to go on the wall showing the extent of environmental problems.

Alternatively, you could ask them to look at English language news on the Internet in different countries and write down countries and environmental or weather problems that are mentioned. They could write notes on any interesting stories they find and bring them to class to talk about.

Grammar – Countable and uncountable nouns

7 Make sure the students understand the concept of countable and uncountable (see Grammar reference, SB page 83). Do the two questions together.

> **Answers**
>
> Countable nouns can be singular or plural.
> Uncountable nouns cannot be plural and take a singular verb.

8 Ask the students in pairs to write the nouns from Exercises 1, 4 and 6 in the lists for countable and uncountable nouns. Check the lists together.

> **Answers**
>
> *Countable:* lake, bushes, mountains, trees, volcanoes, rocks, temperature, season, ocean, hurricane, forests
> *Uncountable:* grass, snow, ice, sky, sunshine, rain, heat, flooding (*flood* is countable)

> See the CD ROM for further practice.

Exam task

🎧 **17** Tell students they are going to think about environmental issues at home and at school. Tell them they will hear a boy talking about how to be environmentally friendly at school and at home. Ask them to predict what he will talk about, putting ideas on the board, e.g.

School: recycling bottles and plastics, using less paper, sending work electronically/by email

Home: turning off lights, taking showers not baths, etc.

Draw their attention to the Exam tip, and tell them that deciding which answers are wrong will help them choose the correct answer. Let them do the Exam task on their own and then correct answers. Play the recording twice.

> **Answers**
>
> 1 B   2 C   3 B   4 A   5 B   6 A   7 C

Recording script CD

You will hear a boy called Tim talking about a school project he has done on the environment. For questions 1–7, choose the best answer (A, B or C).

Teacher: Tim, why did you choose to do your project on 'how to lead a greener life'?

Tim: Well, we'd done a lot about global warming and climate change in our science lessons. It was all a bit complicated really, but I knew something about the big issues. I found it all rather negative and depressing. <u>So, I decided to think small, and see what I could do in my own life, rather than just act completely helpless.</u> And I knew the rest of my family would be interested.

Teacher: Did you find it easy to get information?

Tim: Yeah, I discovered there were lots of people of my age blogging about being green. There was stuff about transport, and ways of getting to school each day. <u>I'd always gone by car – Mum used to drop me off</u> and then drive across town to work. Catching a bus would be better, from the environmental point of view, but we're not on a bus route, so <u>I've gone for riding my bike to school now.</u> Some of my friends live close to the school, so they can walk, but that's not possible for me.

Teacher: OK, and what about being green once you're actually at school?

Tim: Well, I looked up how schools could make better use of resources like paper. I realised that although all school paper was recycled, we used huge quantities, and I thought we should cut down. <u>And then it came to me – it's obvious really – that we should be sending in most of our work electronically, you know, by email attachment. I'm going to recommend it to our school council</u> – the people from each class who give the head teacher suggestions from pupils. I read about something called GOOS paper too, that's paper that's still 'good on one side', and actually most of my friends do that already – use both sides I mean.

Teacher: And what about the school cafeteria?

Tim: We could make that environmentally friendly as well. One school I've read about has 'meatless Mondays'. Apparently, if we eat less meat, we use far less of the world's resources, and animals like cows and sheep pollute the atmosphere with methane gas! It's good to use local produce too, so we don't have to transport it far. That's something our school already does. <u>But we still have machines with bottled milk, water and juice for sale, and I think we should just have jugs of water on the tables instead.</u>

Teacher: Did you think about life at home too?

Tim: Yeah, I think families are high energy consumers, especially now many homes are built with air conditioning. <u>People of my age use huge amounts of power by leaving computer screens and game boxes running 24/7 – they're never turned off! Now that's something we can all do something about!</u> Fortunately, there are improvements like energy-efficient light bulbs though, which most people now have.

Teacher: And what about water? That's a precious resource in every country in the world!

Tim: Absolutely, so we should ask ourselves whether we really need a long hot bath when we get in from playing football! Wouldn't taking a quick shower do? <u>And hands up anyone who leaves the tap on when they brush their teeth. Do you need to do that? Of course you don't. And if you're putting your sports clothes in the washing machine, use a cold setting if you can.</u> Your parents will be happy because you'll use less electricity!

Teacher: Did you think about shopping?

Tim: Yeah, families can do a lot to help the environment and reduce waste when they go to a food store. You don't need a new plastic bag every time you shop. You should take your own bags with you, and buy drinks in a glass bottle if you can, because glass is always recycled. <u>It's better to cut down on food which is packaged,</u> and if you do continue to purchase ready prepared food rather than cooking with fresh ingredients, take the cardboard packets to the recycling bank, don't just chuck them in the dustbin!

Teacher: Thanks Tim.

9 Give students a copy of the recording script (page 81). Ask them in pairs to underline the words that give the answers and highlight the words which show the other answers are wrong. They then discuss with their partner how they got the answer to each question. Get the students to quickly feedback as a class on how they found the task and draw their attention to the other Exam tip.

CLIL Ask students to make a list of all the things their family does at home to be environmentally friendly. Get feedback from the class and discuss whether there is more they could do.

Speaking

Part 3

1 Students sometimes find it hard to come up with the ideas needed to talk about the ideas in Part 3 of the Speaking test. Exercises 1 and 2 are designed to give them the language they need to do this, and the vocabulary from the Listening task they have just done will also be useful.

Remind students that in Part 3 of the exam they will be given some ideas to talk about in relation to a question. Ask them (on their own) to make some notes. They should look at the photos, think about what they heard in the Listening task and add any other ideas they can think of.

2 Remind students that they have to take it in turns to talk about the ideas, and that they can agree, disagree, make a comment or a suggestion as they talk. Ask them in pairs to identify what the phrases are doing. Check answers.

> **Answers**
> 1 I don't really think that's a good idea. – D
> 2 Absolutely. – A
> 3 We all know we shouldn't drop litter. – C
> 4 We could tell everyone to turn off their computers at the end of the lesson. – S
> 5 I don't think turning the heating down would go down well with students here. – C
> 6 I'm with you on that. – A
> 7 That's not what I think, I'm afraid. – D
> 8 What about getting recycling bins in the canteen? – S

Exam task

Tell the students they are going to do the Part 3 task together in pairs. Draw their attention to the Exam tip box.

Give them a minute to look through their notes and phrases again, then ask them to start speaking about the first part of the task (answering the question and discussing the suggestions). Time them for two minutes, perhaps quietly reminding them when they have one minute left. Then ask them to decide which two suggestions would be most successful. Time them for one minute. If they struggle to fill the time, get different pairs to share ideas.

Make a note of any errors or pronunciation problems you hear and correct these at the end. You can also follow up by asking one of the pairs who did the task well to do it again for the class as a whole.

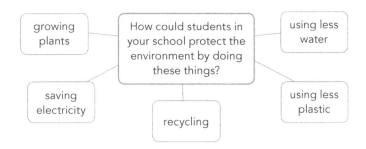

Part 4

Exam task

Remind the students that after they have done Part 3, they will be asked some more general questions related to the same topic in Part 4 of the exam. They have four minutes to do this. Ask the students to take it in turns to ask and answer the questions in the Exam task. Time them, so they get used to how long they have to speak for. At the end you could follow up by correcting any errors or problems you notice. In addition, you can ask a few individual students to feed back their answers to the questions.

Writing

Part 2: Article

1 Check that students understand what an article is. Ask where they would find one: in a newspaper, magazine, or on a website. Show them some examples if possible.

Point out to students that articles can be on a very wide range of topics and that it's important to catch the reader's attention and keep it. Ask them in pairs to look at Exercise 1 and discuss which of the strategies shown would help you to do this.

Answers
1, 2, 4, 6

2 Ask the students to read the article from a school magazine and highlight or underline examples of 1, 2, 4 and 6 in different colours. (Answers below are numbered after the relevant sentence.)

Answers
What I do to be 'green' at home and at school
We all have to do something to help the environment, don't we? [1] I'm only 14 though, so there's no way I personally can do anything about the really big problems, like climate change, is there? [1]

However, I can make sure I live my own life in a green way. It is about making little changes which make a big difference. At home that means not taking baths, because they use too much hot water. [6] (Don't worry, I still take showers!) [2] I turn off the lights and heating in my room when I leave, so I don't waste electricity. [6] I'm very green when it comes to transport too, because I walk everywhere. [6] When I go out with my family we often take the train rather than the car, especially if we want to go into the city, and also it's quicker and parking is expensive. [6]

At school, I help to collect and recycle all the rubbish. That involves collecting everything from the cafeteria. [6] Our head teacher has also decided to turn the central heating on a month later than usual. It's OK, I've put my jumper on! [2]

So I can honestly say that I'm as green as I can be. Are you? [1, 4]

3 Ask the students to compare their answers with a partner, and then discuss the other answers together. Correct as a class.

Answers
The article is in a fairly formal style. Articles will normally be written for a school or college magazine, or for a teenage website, so this is appropriate. They should be lively, catch the reader's attention and give personal opinion and anecdote. It is effective to start with a question (often a tag) in order to involve the reader. It is possible to end with a statement e.g. *Once you start thinking in a green way, it's surprising how many ideas you can come up with.* or a suggestion/comment e.g. *Let's all do what we can to save our planet. / I think we should all do what we can to save the planet.*

4 Ask students to look at the words and phrases underlined in Exercise 2 and check that they understand their meaning. Then ask them in pairs to read the article called 'My favourite time of year' and complete it with the underlined phrases.

Answers
See under 5 below.

5 Ask students to write out the article, giving it a good introduction and a memorable ending. They should put a question in the introduction and add an amusing comment to the main paragraph. Students can work individually, and then read out their articles to their partner.

Show them the model answer below if possible, on the board.

Model answer
My favourite time of year
Don't you just love the summer? Like all young people I adore it, and especially the month of July.
Why do I love July? Most of all (**1**) underline because school has finished and although of course we are really, really sad not to be working at our hot, sweaty desks, that (**2**) underline means going to the beach with my friends, relaxing on the warm sand, swimming and snorkelling. (**3**) underline When it comes to eating out, we often have lunch in a little restaurant on the beach, (**4**) underline especially if we want to meet my aunt and cousins. We always spend the evenings there too; when it's warm, the stars are shining and the music is playing, it's absolute magic. Wouldn't anyone love this experience? For me summer (**5**) underline is about not having any stress or pressure, relaxing and enjoying the sunshine. (**6**) underline However, we sometimes have to travel miles to visit relations who I hardly know, so it isn't all about having fun. Fortunately we get on well for the short time we are together!
I can honestly say that I hope my summers will always be like this. What more could anyone ask for?

Exam task

Ask students to do one of the Exam tasks for homework, and draw their attention to the bullet points.

Model answer

A <u>What I love and hate about the weather in my country.</u>
Do you enjoy hot summers on the beach and cold snowy winters? Well, don't come and live in Holland!
We hardly ever get hot summers, and I hate that. However, the weather is mild throughout the year, and it's easy to get about, even if the skies are grey and it rains quite a lot! You don't get your car stuck in the snow on the way to school, and it's never so hot that you need air-conditioning. That is something I appreciate, even though I wouldn't say I loved it!
As a result of the mild but damp weather, the Dutch people walk and cycle a lot, always with their umbrella and their macs, because we are cheerful people who like being outside.
We do get some cold frosty mornings in winter, and maybe a little sprinkle of snow, and when that happens, I love it. However, the best time in my country is spring. Since the weather is mild and wet, all the flowers come out early and it's beautiful everywhere.
Why don't you come and see for yourself?

B <u>Do you have problems with the environment and pollution in your country?</u>
Water is the big problem in my country, both too much water and too little! Let me explain.
I come from Spain, and like other European countries we have many problems with the environment. In the north, we have experienced heavy storms, with rainfall so heavy that whole campsites have been washed away. This water is very destructive, especially if the rivers get too full and break their banks. The authorities are trying to repair the banks, and to protect them, but it is very hard to do.
Then in the south of my country we have the opposite problem. Some areas have months and even years of drought. The farmers can't grow anything, and soon there won't be enough water for all the houses.
What can we do? There are plans to take salt water from the sea and turn it into fresh water, and another obvious answer is that we must find a way to get all the water in the north down to the south, where it is needed.
If you know a way to do it, please tell my government!

See the Writing Extra in the Workbook for more exercises on writing articles.

Wildlife

Reading and Use of English

Part 6

1 Students write down their answers and then compare them.

Answers

A Siberian tiger: Russia, China and North Korea
B White rhino: Central and southern Africa
C Humpback whale: They are found around the world (e.g. off the coasts of Canada, Iceland, Japan, Mexico, Caribbean), and they migrate up to 25,000 km a year.

2 Students work in groups to note down some facts about the animals. You may need to prompt them or give them time to look up some information (see CLIL activity).

Suggested answers

Whales eat fish, white rhinos eat grass and Siberian tigers eat other animals.
Both whales and white rhinos tend to travel in groups but Siberian tigers live alone.
Rhinos enjoy the hot sun whereas Siberian tigers live in colder climates.
Rhinos live on grassland but Siberian tigers prefer woods and forests.
Both whales and rhinos like water. Rhinos like to be in muddy pools, whereas whales swim in the ocean.

3 The main point here is that the animals are endangered so attract attention.

Suggested answers

They're beautiful, they attract tourists, people photograph them a lot, they're endangered (all three are rare animals that could become extinct. They are on the WWF Red List of endangered animals.).

CLIL Students can work in groups and look at the WWF website to find out more about one of these animals or another endangered animal. They can draw up a fact file about it. What are the advantages of saving it, e.g. for the environment and tourism?

4 This task gets students to focus on the importance of linking words and expressions. Ask students to read the text and the three sentences. The three sentences are almost identical apart from the linking words – *Because of this*, *Therefore* and *however*. Talk about why A and B don't fit. A and B both start with words which suggest that there is a positive connection between the elephants' huge ears and the sounds the elephants produce whereas C contrasts the two sentences and doesn't suggest the ears and the sounds are connected. They all connect to the sentence which follows. Point out to students that it is really important to read both before and after the gap as more than one sentence might connect with what goes after it, but only one will connect with the words before (and vice versa). Draw attention to the Exam tip.

Answer

C

Exam task

Give students ten minutes to do the Exam task individually. Check whether they have finished and give them another five minutes if needed. Ask them to work in pairs to compare their answers.

Answers

1 C   2 D   3 G   4 B   5 F   6 A

5 Students discuss in pairs. When they have finished, conduct a class discussion.

Reading and Use of English

Part 2

Grammar – Articles

1 Ask the students to read the information about articles in the Grammar reference, SB page 83, and complete the sentences. Check the answers together.

> **Answers**
> 1 a *or* an   2 the   3 the   4 no article   5 no article   6 the

2 Get students to work in pairs to decide which of the place names need *the* in front of them, and write them next to the correct heading. Ask them to add more examples to the list if they can. (They could use an atlas or the Internet to help them.)

> **Answers**
> *Oceans, seas and rivers:* the Amazon, the Atlantic Ocean, the Thames
> *Regions:* the Far East, the north of England
> *Countries with the word republic, kingdom, states:* the Czech Republic, the United Kingdom, the United States
> *Deserts and mountain ranges:* the Himalayas, the Sahara
>
> **NB** The following do not need *the* in front of them: California, Lake Como, Italy, London, South America

3 Get students to do Exercise 3 alone or in pairs.

> **Answers**
> 1 a; the   2 a; the   3 a; the   4 the; a   5 the

4 Students should do Exercise 4 alone or in pairs.

> **Answers**
> 1 –   2 the   3 the   4 –

5 Ask students to do the exercise alone, and then check it with a partner. This exercise relates to all the grammar on articles in the Grammar reference, SB page 83.

> **Answers**
> 1 the   2 the   3 –   4 an   5 a   6 the   7 –   8 The   9 –   10 –
> 11 –   12 a   13 –   14 The   15 –   16 the   17 the   18 the
> 19 the   20 the

> See the Workbook for an exercise on countable and uncountable nouns.

Grammar – *so* and *such* (*a/an*)

6 Ask the students to do the exercise in pairs, and then complete the rules below.

> **Answers**
> 1 such   2 so   3 such   4 such   5 so   6 so
> Rules: such; so

Grammar – *too* and *enough*

7 Ask students to look at the cartoons and write a sentence about each using the prompt words. Correct their answers and then refer them to the appropriate section in the Grammar reference, SB page 83.

> **Answers**
> 1 He hasn't got / doesn't have enough money.
> 2 The hill is too steep (for her).
> 3 There is too much food (for him).
> 4 The suitcase isn't big enough (for all the clothes / for all his things).

> See the Workbook and CD ROM for more practice on *so/such* and *too/enough*.

Exam task

Make sure that students know the words *penguin* and *backpack*. Check they know where and how penguins normally live. (In the Antarctic. They are used to cold weather and live on fish.)

Move on to the Part 2 task and draw the students' attention to the Exam tip. Give them ten minutes to do the task and check their answers with a partner.

> **Answers**
> 1 only   2 ago   3 too   4 when   5 the   6 there   7 where   8 so

8 Students discuss their answers with a partner. Ask them to explain their reasons for choosing an answer if it differs from their partner's. This should encourage them to think more carefully about their answers.

7 People and style

Unit objectives

FIRST FOR SCHOOLS TOPICS	shopping and fashion, people and feelings
GRAMMAR	verbs and expressions followed by *to* or *-ing*, reported speech
VOCABULARY	shopping, clothes, feelings, personality
READING AND USE OF ENGLISH	Part 4: reported speech Part 5: reading the options in detail
WRITING	Part 2 letter and email: describing and giving information
LISTENING	Part 3: listening for words and expressions with similar meanings
SPEAKING	Part 1: expressing likes and dislikes Part 2: talking about advantages and disadvantages, hesitating

Shopping and fashion

Listening

Part 3

1 Ask students to work in pairs to choose words and expressions. Add more vocabulary if appropriate.

> **Answers**
>
> A elegant, expensive-looking, formal, smart
> B individual, outrageous, second-hand, stylish, vintage
> C casual, comfortable, everyday

2 Students work in groups to talk about clothes and fashions. Have a class discussion.

3 🎧 18 Play the recording. Students think about the questions and discuss the answers with a partner.

> **Answer**
>
> She is in photo B.

> **Recording script**
>
> | Teenage girl: | I'm obsessed with keeping up with the latest trends. I like to stand out. I tend to wear outrageous clothes rather than more conventional ones. But they have to suit me and look really cool. As soon as something goes out of fashion, I stop wearing it. But I don't throw old clothes away as they sometimes come back into fashion. I know people who have loads of money and show off by wearing designer labels but I think you can look just as good in cheaper stuff. |
> |---|---|

4 🎧 18 In this part of the listening paper, there is a lot of distraction which has to be discounted in order to get the right answer. It is important that students listen for expressions which mean the same as the options in the

question. Play the recording again, pausing it after each sentence so students can write down what they hear.

> **Answers**
>
> 1 be passionate about – obsessed with
> 2 staying in touch with – keeping up with
> 3 look different – stand out
> 4 slightly shocking – outrageous
> 5 fairly typical – conventional
> 6 look good on me – suit me
> 7 becomes unfashionable – goes out of fashion
> 8 get rid of – throw away
> 9 become fashionable again – come back into fashion
> 10 be very rich – have loads of money
> 11 draw attention to yourself – show off
> 12 clothes by particular designers – designer labels

Exam task

🎧 19 Read the instructions together, give students 30 seconds to read the questions (this is how long they have in the exam), then play the recording twice. You may like to give the students a copy of the script to look at while you go through the answers (page 82).

> **Answers**
>
> 1 E Ask why F is wrong (she likes to have her friends' opinions but she doesn't say she dresses like them) and why G is wrong (she knows what to buy when she has money but she doesn't say she spends a lot)
> 2 F Ask why A is wrong (he says he's not adventurous but not that he has a preference) and why B is wrong (he might keep up with the fashions when he has more money but not now)
> 3 A Ask why F is wrong (she likes shopping with her friend but they have different tastes) and why H is wrong (her mum likes her to look smart but that isn't so important to her)
> 4 C Ask why A is wrong (he sometimes wears unusual colours but not necessarily the same ones) and why D is wrong (the fashions change quickly but his tastes don't change quickly – in fact he spends a long time looking for what he wants)
> 5 H Ask why A is wrong (she won't wear colours that don't match but she doesn't say she prefers certain colours) and why F is wrong (she takes more care about her appearance than her friends)

> **Recording script**
>
> *You will hear five people talking about shopping for clothes. For questions 1–5, choose from the list (A–H) what each speaker says. Use the letters only once. There are three extra letters which you do not need to use.*
>
> *Speaker 1*
>
> There isn't much to do round here at weekends, so I usually go to the shopping centre with my friends. We go in loads of shops and try stuff on, it's all too expensive for us but it's something to do. Most of it looks really bad on me as I'm really tall and thin but I've got used to what kind of clothes look good on me – things like long jumpers and skinny jeans. So when I've got some money, I know exactly what to look for. I like to have my friends with me though for a second opinion.

Speaker 2

Most of my friends want to get all the latest stuff but I never really know what to buy. So when I go to get something new, <u>I try to get what my mates are wearing.</u> Mostly we wear jeans and hoodies and, if we can afford them, designer T-shirts. They never really go out of fashion. I like going round the shops and looking at what's there but I'm not good at deciding and I'm not very adventurous with colours and styles. When I've got a lot of money, then I might decide to keep up with the latest fashions.

Speaker 3

My mum and my sister and I often go shopping together. We have a good time, especially if my mum is feeling generous, but she obviously likes different things from me. <u>She thinks I should wear bright cheerful things, whereas I like to wear grey or black.</u> She also thinks that being well-dressed is really important, so I should buy things that look smart and will last but I prefer to buy cheap clothes I can replace. I love going shopping with my best friend, too. We've got completely different tastes but we like getting each other's opinions all the same.

Speaker 4

It annoys me that all the shops have the same things in them, then the fashion suddenly changes and one day everybody's wearing long shorts and then the next day the latest thing is tight black jeans. Some styles really suit some people but not others, so it doesn't really work. I usually go shopping on my own because I find most of the chain stores a bit boring and <u>I'm looking for stuff that will make me look different from my friends.</u> I do find it eventually – sometimes it's just an unusual colour but often I invent my own fashion. Some of it might look a bit strange but I don't mind.

Speaker 5

I've been interested in clothes since I was little, when I used to argue with my mum about what I would wear – I used to refuse to wear colours that didn't match and I'm still the same. I take ages to get ready in the morning because <u>I want to look stylish and elegant.</u> It's not because I want people to notice me but because I feel better about myself when I've taken a bit of time. My friends like to get dressed up in their best clothes when they go out but the rest of the time they just wear jeans and a T-shirt. That's not for me.

CLIL Get students to find information about current fashions on the Internet. They could look at fashions in different English-speaking countries, so all the information they find is in English, e.g. Britain, USA, Canada, South Africa, Australia, New Zealand, Singapore, India. Ask them to make notes, or do drawings/download pictures and compare what they find. Are the same colours and clothes fashionable in different countries? They could simply discuss their findings, or produce posters on 'Fashion in Different Countries' for a wall display. They could also compare the fashion in any of the countries with fashion in their own country.

See the Workbook for a vocabulary exercise on shopping.

Speaking

Part 1

1 🎧 20 Play the recording. Students make brief notes. Play the recording again so they can complete their notes and check the answers. Students should notice that the speakers expanded their answers to give more information or an opinion. This will gain them marks.

Answers

	Like	Dislike	Neither like or dislike
Sofia	music, playing guitar, singing, skiing, beach	mountains in summer, long walks, looking at the views	
Daniel	watching football (Barcelona), history and geography	playing football and other sports	English, science

Recording script

Examiner:	What do you like doing in your free time, Sofia?
Sofia:	I'm really into music, so I spend a lot of time playing the guitar and I enjoy singing. I attempt to play some of the songs from my favourite bands and one day I hope to be in a band myself.
Examiner:	Daniel, do you like sports?
Daniel:	I'm mad about football, of course, like everyone who comes from Barcelona. I love going to see them when they play at home.
Examiner:	And do you play any sports?
Daniel:	I'm not very keen on playing football myself. I prefer to watch it. And I don't really like playing other sports very much either.
Examiner:	Sofia, what do you like to do when you're on holiday?
Sofia:	I live near the sea so we usually go to the mountains for holidays. I'm very keen on skiing. I love to spend time out on the snow. I first learnt when I was four years old, so I'm quite good at it now.
Examiner:	What about summer holidays?
Sofia:	I'm not that interested in going to the mountains in the summer. I can't bear going for long walks and looking at the views. I suppose it's because my parents made me do it when I was little. I prefer being at the beach.
Examiner:	What's your favourite subject at school, Daniel?
Daniel:	Well, English is OK but it's not my favourite. History and geography are what I enjoy most. I don't mind doing science but I'm not very good at the practical stuff – the experiments. I'd prefer to study things like the history of science. I want to study history at university. I'd like to be a history teacher one day.

2 🎧 `20` Play the recording again and ask students to fill in the gaps. Stop the recording to give them time to write. Students now have a list of expressions they can use in the Exam task below.

Answers

Like (✓)	Dislike (✗)	Neither like or dislike (?)
I'm <u>really into</u> music.	I'm <u>not very keen on</u> playing football myself.	Well, English is OK but it's <u>not my favourite</u>.
I <u>enjoy</u> singing.	I <u>don't really like</u> playing other sports very much.	I <u>don't mind</u> doing science.
I'm <u>mad about</u> football, of course.	I'm <u>not that interested</u> in going to the mountains in the summer.	
I <u>love</u> going to see them.	I <u>can't bear</u> going for long walks.	
I'm <u>very keen on</u> skiing.		
History and geography are <u>what I enjoy most</u>.		

Exam task

Students practise in pairs, asking each other the questions in their books. They should use a range of expressions to express their likes and dislikes. Point out that in the exam if they don't say much, the examiner will ask a question to help like *Why?* so they should help their partner if necessary.

Grammar – Verbs and expressions followed by *to* infinitive or *-ing* form

3 Ask students to put the verbs and expressions in the correct column and check the answers.

Answers

to- infinitive	*-ing* form	either to- infinitive or *-ing* form
attempt	can't bear	like
hope	don't mind	love
want	enjoy	prefer
would like	be interested in	
would prefer	be keen on	
agree (Ex 4)	look forward to (Ex 4)	
	suggest (Ex 4)	
	imagine (Ex4)	

4 Students do the exercise in pairs and then add the verbs *agree, look forward to, suggest* and *imagine* to the correct columns in the table.

In the Grammar reference, SB page 84, there are more verbs which students should learn to use correctly.

> See the Workbook and CD ROM for further practice on verbs and expressions with *to* or *-ing*.

Answers

1 to come   2 seeing   3 to see   4 to come   5 to go   6 going
7 living   8 to go   9 to buy   10 playing

Part 2

5 The photos can be used for a discussion about how the students prefer to shop. You can also ask them about the rest of their family.

6 🎧 `21` Play the recording of a student talking about two of the photos. Students listen to identify the photos and tick the ideas he mentions.

Answers

He talks about the bottom two photos.
Advantages: lots of choice, compare prices, convenient, you can try clothes on, more fun
Disadvantages: quite traditional, not much for teenagers, can't try things on, wait for the post

Recording script

Adam: In both photos people are shopping. Mmm ... let me see ... In the first picture, someone's shopping on the Internet. Err ... well ... this has lots of advantages because there's loads to choose from and you can compare prices. It's also really convenient as you can do it at home. The second picture on the other hand shows people shopping in the main street, maybe in a small town. Let me think for a moment ... The shops look quite traditional and maybe there isn't too much there for people of my age. The advantage is that you can see what you are buying and try clothes on, whereas you can't do that on the Internet and, er, you have to wait for your purchases to arrive in the post. Not everyone would agree but ... I think that we need both ways of shopping because sometimes it's fun just to go out into the town when you want something.

7 Ask students to complete the expressions. Play the recording again if you need to.

> **Answers**
> 1 Mmm, let me see
> 2 Let me think for a moment
> 3 Not everyone would agree but I think

8 Students make notes of other things they could say about Adam's photographs.

9 Work as a class and write ideas on the board about the other two photographs.

Exam task

Students work in pairs and choose two photographs each (each pair should choose one of the photos that Adam talked about and pair it with one of the others). Remind them they are going to compare the photographs and talk about the advantages and disadvantages. Look at the expressions they can use for comparing and ask if they can add any others – remind them of comparisons (*There are far more … ., The … isn't as …*, etc.). Time the pairs while they speak for a minute each and then ask a few students a follow-up question (*Do you like shopping? Who do you usually shop with? Where do you go shopping? What is your favourite shop?* etc.). Look at the Exam tip together.

> **CLIL** Students could find out information about shopping centres in different countries, and what facilities they have. Alternatively, you could find the information for them on the Internet and simply give them the information. Students could then compare the shopping centres, looking for similarities and differences. This could be done as a group speaking exercise, or as a writing task.

People and feelings

Writing

Part 2: Letter and email

1 Read the Exam task with students and point out that they have to write about a **famous** person, but that as the question doesn't specify, the person could be alive or dead. Tell them that they have to write about how they **admire** the person, so they can't write anything negative.

Check that they all know about Nelson Mandela. Brainstorm what they know about him and put it on the board.

Then ask students to read Anna's response, and in pairs to complete the letter with the words and phrases. These will help to link the letter together well.

2 Ask them to highlight the adjectives used to describe Nelson Mandela's personality, and check the meaning of any adjectives they don't know with a dictionary.

Answers to Exercises 1 and 2 (personality adjectives in bold)

> Hi Lauren,
> You asked me to tell you about a famous person I admire. Well, that's easy! (1) <u>Nobody could impress me</u> more than Nelson Mandela!
> He is (2) <u>famous for being</u> the first black president of South Africa, and for being (3) <u>the man who</u> brought freedom to his people. (4) <u>Despite</u> spending 27 years in prison, he never got **discouraged**. He (5) <u>managed to</u> keep smiling, stay **optimistic** and be **cheerful**. He never, ever gave up. He was amazingly **confident** and (6) <u>as a result</u> of this belief in himself, he achieved the most amazing things.
> (7) <u>Even though</u> he was fighting a very cruel system, he was always **patient**, **polite** and **thoughtful** to those around him. He was originally a lawyer, and (8) <u>even</u> some of the warders in the prison admired him.
> There is (9) <u>one other quality which</u> I really like. If you look at the photos and videos of him, you can see he was always laughing and smiling. There are photos of him dancing and meeting famous singers and film stars when he was president. He loved life and music! He (10) <u>comes across as</u> such a great guy! I wish I had met him.

3 Give the students a minute to think about a famous person they would like to write about. Then get them to answer the questions in pairs. **NB** You could also ask them to look up some information about a famous person for homework before the lesson, so they have some facts ready.

4 When they have prepared some notes about their famous person, go through the bullet points with them. For the first point, elicit opening and endings for letters and put them on the board.

- Openings: Dear Lauren, Hi Lauren, Hello Lauren
- Endings: *I hope that's everything you wanted to know. / That's all I have time for now.*
  Write to me again soon, / Best wishes, / Love

Finally, draw students' attention to the fact that the letter is about describing and giving information; there is no space in 140–190 words for 'chat'. Ask them to look back at the letters from Lauren and Anna and say whether they are formal or informal in style. They are fairly formal, because they are requesting and giving information which can be used in a school project. Anna has also been enthusiastic in her reply. Ask for examples of this. (The opening and ending of the letter, which have sentences with exclamation marks.) This is very appropriate for the question, because you have to write about someone famous that you admire. Students should be encouraged to write in a similar style, and avoid slang and very informal expressions.

Students should now write their own answers in class. They can check their letters with a partner before handing them in.

5 Ask students to choose someone in their own family they admire, and a student in the college.

1 Students discuss and explain their choice(s) in pairs.

2 They write down any relevant adjectives they can use.

3 Students can then do one Exam task for homework.

Exam task

Model answers

1

Dear Andrew,

You asked me to write and tell you about the person I admire most in my family. It's definitely my mother.

She always manages to be cheerful, and she's very patient with my little brothers and me. She never gets discouraged, even when we do badly at school, and somehow she gets us organised so we can sort things out for ourselves. She's thoughtful too, so we always get birthday presents that we really like, and at weekends we have fun with her and dad, just going to the beach near us, or having friends round.

Mum has a job. She's a manager in the local supermarket, so she works hard. Despite having very little time for herself while we were young, she's done very well, and she got promotion quickly. I think she gives us a very good example of how you can be successful if you work hard and make the most of your time.

As you can see, I'm lucky to have a mum like this, and my brothers think so too.

I hope that answers your question.

Best wishes

Tim

2

Dear Julia,

You wanted me to write and tell you about a student in my college that I admire. I'm not going to tell you about someone who is the cleverest person in the school, or the best at sport, or even the best looking.

I'm going to tell you about Robbie, who comes to school every day in his wheelchair. I've known him since he was at primary school, and he has been in his chair for three years now.

He's grown up knowing that this was how his life would turn out, and he just gets on with things. He's absolutely brilliant with computers – better than some of the teachers I think – and he's decided that he wants a career with a computer company. His attitude is so positive that I'm sure he will succeed. He's very artistic, and enjoys drawing. He's also very funny, and he tries not to take his problems too seriously.

As a result, we all like him, and we look after him if he needs help.

I hope that answers your question.

Love

Jo

Reading and Use of English

Part 5

1 This short text practises one kind of question that often appears in Part 5. Ask students to read the text and tick as many adjectives as they think apply. If they don't know any of them, they should look them up as they are common adjectives at B2 level.

> **Answers**
>
> annoyed, angry, furious, irritated (possibly upset)

2 Write these questions on the board and get students to underline the parts of the text which give the answers:

Did Olivia arrive late? (Yes – 'the crowded room' and 'Then she noticed the birthday cake')

Does the writer find it difficult to make friends? (We know that he had friends 'I was standing with my friends' but we don't know if he found it difficult to make friends)

Did Olivia deliberately ignore the writer? (Yes – 'She turned her head and walked right on')

Why didn't the writer speak to Olivia? (He was angry with her 'That wouldn't have been a good idea while I was so mad at her')

Then ask students to choose the correct multiple choice answer. Read the Exam tip together.

> **Answers**
>
> C
>
> Ask them how many of the adjectives that they ticked in 1 are in the options.
>
> Ask why A is wrong (he was irritated but because Olivia ignored him, not because she was late)
>
> Ask why B is wrong (he was angry but not because he didn't make friends easily)
>
> Ask why D is wrong (he didn't speak to Olivia because he was angry, not because he didn't have the confidence)

3 Give students three minutes to read the text quickly.

4 Students do the task individually and then compare their answers in pairs. Tell them not to worry about vocabulary they don't know as there will always be words and expressions in this part that they can guess the meaning of or don't need to understand.

Exam task

> **Answers**
>
> 1 B 2 D 3 B 4 C 5 D 6 A

Reading and Use of English

Part 4

Grammar – Reported speech

1 If students need to revise reported speech, look at the Grammar reference, SB page 84, together first. If they don't need to, direct them to it at the end of the lesson.

> **Answers**
>
> 1 was 2 seemed 3 was feeling 4 had lived 5 would have to
> 6 had been shopping (*was shopping* also possible)
> 7 had gone 8 had seen 9 was 10 cheer up 11 wanted
> 12 needed

2 Build up the table together on the board after students have underlined the verbs in the speech bubbles and the exercise.

> **Answers**
>
> | Tense in direct speech | Tense in reported speech |
> |---|---|
> | present simple | past simple |
> | present continuous | past continuous |
> | present perfect simple | past perfect simple |
> | *will* | *would* |
> | past continuous | past perfect continuous |
> | past simple | past perfect simple |

3 Get students to write the two reported questions and talk about the difference between them (see Grammar reference, SB page 84).

> **Answers**
>
> The girl's mum asked her how she was.
> The girl's mum asked if she wanted to go shopping. (We use *come* when we ask someone to join us in doing something but when we report the sentence, *come* changes to *go*.)
> We use *if* when we report a *yes*/*no* question.

4 Students should complete these sentences to check they have understood.

> **Answers**
>
> 1 why he was so late.
> 2 what she was watching.
> 3 if he had scored a goal.
> 4 if there was any food left.
> 5 when he would be home.
> 6 if she had seen his bag.

5 These common reporting verbs are often tested in Use of English Part 4.

> **Answers**
>
> *advised*, *asked*, *encouraged*, *persuaded*, *reminded*, *told* and *warned* fit the gap. The verbs which don't fit the gap are *agreed*, *explained*, *mentioned* and *said*. *Agree* isn't followed directly by an object like *her*, and *said*, *explained* and *mentioned* would be followed by *to her*.

6 Get students to complete the exercise individually. They can then compare their answers with a partner.

> **Answers**
>
> 1 reminded 2 agreed 3 warned 4 mention

7 This exercise tests the difference between *said*, *told* and *asked* (see Grammar reference SB page 84). Go back to Exercise 1 and ask students to underline *said*, *told* and *asked* and the words which follow them. Ask them what they notice. We say: *She said (that)* ... or *She said to her* but not ~~*She said her*~~; *She told her (that)* but not ~~*She told (that)* ...~~; *She asked (her) (if)* or *She asked her to* ... but not ~~*She asked to her*~~.

> **Answers**
>
> 1 said 2 told 3 asked 4 told 5 told 6 asked 7 told them
> 8 asked

Exam task

Before students look at the Exam task, write the example on the board with the two possible answers below and ask students why B is wrong:

I stopped learning to play the drums because the neighbours complained.

GAVE

The neighbours complained about the drums .... learning to play them.

A *so I gave up*
B *although I gave up*

(Both answers use the word *gave* and use fewer than five words but A is correct and B is wrong. B doesn't mean the same as the first sentence because it says the neighbours continued to complain.)

Read the Exam tip with the class before they complete the exercise.

> **Answers**
>
> 1 it was picked up by
> 2 told her not to
> 3 Does anyone know how
> 4 such a long film
> 5 would have lent
> 6 us not to go

> See the Workbook and CD ROM for further practice on reported speech.

8 Keeping up to date

Unit objectives

FIRST FOR SCHOOLS TOPICS	science, technology
GRAMMAR	relative clauses
VOCABULARY	science, computers, equipment
READING AND USE OF ENGLISH	Part 3: word building Part 7: ignoring distraction
WRITING	Part 1 essay: linking, vocabulary, conclusions
LISTENING	Part 1: identifying the situation
SPEAKING	Part 3: moving the conversation forward, using varied vocabulary Part 4: discussing the effects of technology

Science

Reading and Use of English

Part 7

1 Talk about what subject the students in the photos are studying and what they are doing, writing some vocabulary on the board.

Photo 1: Ecology/Biology/Geography – They are carrying out a survey / investigating wildlife, clean water, river flow, etc.

Photo 2: Maths/Physics – They are doing calculations and solving equations.

Photo 3: Chemistry – They are measuring substances in test tubes.

2 Students work in pairs to add the topics to the columns (all these words are B2 except *fractions* and *geometry*). Ask students what they are studying in science at the moment so they can add any other useful words.

> **Answers**
> Ecology: ecosystems, endangered species, pollution, recycling
> Biology: cells, diseases, ecosystems, endangered species, genetics, plants
> Chemistry: gases, plastics
> Physics: electricity, heat, light, mirrors, sound
> Mathematics: fractions, geometry, percentages

3 Have a class discussion about the importance of science and how popular it is.

Exam task

Read the Exam tip together. Give students ten minutes to do the task and then get them to compare their answers.

> **Answers**
> 1 A 2 B 3 D 4 C 5 B 6 A 7 D 8 C 9 D 10 B

CLIL Students could work in groups to look at a 'Young Scientist Award' website and find an invention they are interested in. Each group could present their invention to the class with pictures. The class could vote on the best invention.

Writing

Part 1: Essay

Grammar – Relative clauses

1 In pairs students complete the sentences with the correct relative pronoun. They can look at the Grammar reference, SB page 85, if they need to.

> **Answers**
> 1 who 2 which 3 which 4 whose 5 which 6 who

2 Ask students to continue in their pairs and discuss the questions. Go over the answers.

> **Answers**
> 1 You can omit the relative pronoun in 3 as it is not the subject of the verb which follows it ('other kids' is the subject of 'have covered'). In sentences 1 and 2 the relative pronoun is the subject of the verb which follows, so you can't omit the relative pronoun.
> 2 You can put *that* in 1, 2 and 3 (all defining clauses). You cannot use *that* in non-defining clauses.
> 3 A non-defining clause has commas around it, a defining clause does not.

3 Ask the students to read the essay on studying science and in pairs to put in the missing relative pronouns. They should also say whether *that* or *no pronoun* are possible alternatives.

> **Answers**
> 1 which / that
> 2 whose
> 3 which / that / –
> 4 which / that / –
> 5 who
> 6 which
> 7 which
> 8 who / that

> See the Workbook for further practice on relative clauses.

4 Ask the students to look at two possible endings for the essay. Get them to discuss in pairs whether both are suitable and say why/why not.

> **Answers**
> A doesn't fit. It contradicts what the student wrote in paragraphs 1 and 2.
> B fits well. It follows logically from what the student wrote in paragraphs 1 and 2, and uses an example from the student's own country, which is a good idea.

5 Remind the students that it is always important to plan an essay before you start writing. Get students to work in pairs and complete the plan for the essay. You could check the answers by getting one pair to put their plan on the board.

If possible, show the completed essay below on the board, and ask students to look at the phrases underlined and explain how they help to link the essay together. There is a follow-up exercise to this in the Writing Extra in the Workbook.

> **Suggested answers**
>
> Paragraph 1: good for everyone to study science (important subject), good to study till 18 if *you like science and want a career in science*
> Paragraph 2: *not good if you are weak in science – difficult for teachers; frustrating for bad students*
> Paragraph 3: *system in own country; everyone studies till 16, then they can choose*
> Conclusion: *everyone needs to study science, but till 18 is too long; 16 is better.*
>
> **Completed essay**
> I certainly agree that all students should study science at school. It's a subject which is incredibly important in our world today. However, I think the issue of how long students should study it is more difficult. If you are the kind of student whose main interest is to become a doctor or a physicist, then certainly you will want to study science until you are 18. You will probably enjoy it too, because science is the subject that you are interested in, and probably the one which you are good at.
> But less able students, who find it difficult to pass exams in physics, biology and chemistry, will not be enthusiastic. These subjects, which can be hard at higher levels, may prove too challenging for them. The students will then get very frustrated with science, which means they will behave badly in class. That will make things very difficult for the teachers that are responsible for them.
> In my country, students study science until they are 16, and then choose whatever subjects they like until they are 18. I think this is a good system. I would therefore like to conclude by saying that I do not agree with the idea that all students should study science until the age of 18.

6 In pairs, students discuss the phrases. Check answers as a class.

> **Answers**
> 1 E 2 B 3 B 4 E 5 E 6 B

7 Point out to students the need to use a range of vocabulary if they want to get a good mark on an essay. Ask them in pairs to choose the correct verbs for the essay on global warming, using a dictionary to help if necessary.

> **Answers**
> 1 discovered 2 argue 3 claim 4 warned 5 say 6 think
> 7 encourage 8 disagree

8 Ask students to continue working in pairs and discuss the questions.

Students can discuss question 3 in pairs or small groups and you can finish with a brief class discussion. Elicit and put on the board the problems that students are optimistic about, and those they are pessimistic about, as a summary of the discussion.

> **Answers**
> 1 Three
> 2 Yes, the student talks about both the points given, then adds his own view (that governments need to act and spend money on the problem). He then reaches a clear conclusion; he is optimistic about the future and disagrees with the statement.
> 3 Students' personal views.

9 Get students to make a list of any of the vocabulary and phrases in the essay that they could use in an essay of their own about global warming.

CLIL Students could be asked to find examples on the Internet of the ways some global warming problems are being dealt with successfully for homework and report back at the start of the next lesson. (This gives practice in using the phrases and vocabulary.)

Exam task

Ask students to do the Exam task as homework. Remind them that they can use ideas, vocabulary and linking phrases from the unit.

> **Model answer**
> Do you think in future it will be possible for robots to become doctors and teachers?
> I certainly think that robots have a big part to play in the future of medicine. In many hospitals, robots are already being used to perform operations because they are far more accurate than human beings. However, robots do not work alone. Their 'hands' are used, but they are always controlled by human surgeons. Also, it's always human doctors and nurses who talk to the patients and deal with their worries.
> As for robots being teachers, I think this is impossible. A teacher needs to communicate with students and encourage them, and a robot simply cannot do this. Robots might be able to help with simple tasks like marking homework, but they will never be able to replace teachers in the classroom because they cannot deal with pupils' questions or feelings.
> I think these two examples give a clear answer to the question. In my personal opinion, humans will increasingly work with robots which will do the technical tasks. However, robots cannot work alone; they always need a human master. I would like to conclude by saying that I am pleased about this. I would not like people to be replaced by machines.

> See the Writing Extra in the Workbook for more exercises on writing essays.

Technology

Reading and Use of English
Part 3

Vocabulary – Computers

1 Some of the vocabulary might be the same in the students' own language but check they understand any that isn't. Add any other useful words that students might want to use when talking about computers.

Answers

1/2 update / spreadsheet   3 log out   4 email   5 browser
6 webcam

2 Ask students to work in pairs to complete the gaps.

Answers

1 drive   2 back   3 data   4 password   5 log   6 bookmark
7 installed   8 applications

Vocabulary – Word building (3)

3 This introduces the word-building exercise. Do the first part
of the exercise as a class. Then ask students to complete the
table and check with a partner. These are common affixes.

Answers

application   attachment   automatically   easily   powerful

Verb	Noun	Adjective	Adverb
disable *enable*	*disability* *ability*	able *unable* *disabled*	*ably*
	commerce	*commercial*	*commercially*
compete	*competition* *competitor*	*competitive* *uncompetitive*	*competitively* *uncompetitively*

4 Students look at the table to complete the lists. Refer them
to the Exam tip.

Answers

To make nouns, add -*ity, -tion, -or*
To make adjectives, add -*d, -al, -ive*

5 Students read the text first to decide what part of speech is
required in each gap. They don't try to complete the gaps
yet.

Answers

1 adverb   2 adjective   3 noun   4 noun   5 noun   6 noun
7 adverb   8 adjective   9 noun   10 adjective

6 They now use the affixes provided to make a new word for
each gap.

Answers

2 technological   3 ability   4 popularity   5 weight
6 development   7 actually   8 unrecognisable   9 competition
10 powerful

7 Students practise making negatives. They have made a
word with a prefix in gap 8. Ask them to look back at the
other words in the gaps to see if they can make any others
negative.

Answers

Unrecognisable has the prefix; others which can be made
negative: *inability, unpopularity*

8 Ask students to make more negative words. There is a rule
for when we use *im-, ir-* and *il-*. Ask them if they know
what it is (*im*- is usually used before words beginning with
p and *m*, *ir*- is usually used before a word beginning with

r, and *il*- before a word beginning with *l*). These are much
less common than *un-, in-* or *dis-*.

Answers

disapproval   inexperienced   unfortunate   dishonesty
illegal   impatient   impolite   unreliable   irresponsible
dissatisfied   misunderstanding

See the Workbook and CD ROM for more practice on word-
building.

Exam task

Before students begin, ask them what their strategy will be
(read for meaning and to think about which part of speech
is needed in each space, fill in their answers, read the whole
text again for meaning).

Answers

1 dramatic   2 Initially   3 permission   4 illegally   5 strength
6 passionate   7 knowledge   8 helpful

Speaking

Part 3

1 Ask students to look at the pictures and answer the
questions in pairs. Remind them to give reasons for their
answers.

2 🎧 **22** Draw students' attention to the question the
students on the recording have to answer. Look at questions
1–4 and tell students they are going to listen to how the
students communicate with each other which will help
them keep their own conversations moving.

Answers

1 Yes
2 Yes
3 No
4 Yes

Recording script	
Examiner:	Now, I'd like you to talk about something together for about two minutes. I'd like you to talk about how important some inventions are in our daily lives. Here are some different inventions. All right?
Karolina:	Shall I begin?
Miguel:	OK.
Karolina:	Well, I use my laptop every day for my homework and for fun too – I watch films on it and listen to music.
Miguel:	Yes, it's the same for me. But computers are also crucial for most people at work and for everything really. Nothing would work without computers.
Karolina:	What about the fridge?
Miguel:	Food wouldn't last so long without a fridge. But we could live without it I suppose – it's not so essential.

Karolina:	And people would have to go shopping every day so they might waste less food. But they are vital in very hot countries, of course.
Miguel:	Yeah, you're right. And we couldn't live without cars, could we? I can't wait to learn to drive. It's so annoying having to get the bus everywhere.
Karolina:	Don't you think we ought to try to be less dependent on cars though?
Miguel:	That's not going to happen, is it? Lots of people like cycling but I don't think bicycles are a basic necessity in the same way as a car.
Karolina:	I agree, although I think in some countries they are more important as a way of travelling. Most people live in cities though, and cycling can be dangerous in traffic.
Miguel:	The last thing to talk about is a TV. What do you think about that?
Karolina:	Well, it's not so significant now because you can watch TV on your computer or even your phone.
Miguel:	But you can't sit down and watch a film with friends on a phone. It's too small!
Karolina:	That's true.
Miguel:	I would miss my TV. I like lying on the sofa in front of it when I'm tired.

3 🎧 22 Get students to listen to the student discussion again and write down their answers to questions 1–4. Get them to check in pairs before correcting as a class. Read through the Exam tip with the students.

> **Answers**
> 1 Shall I begin?
> 2 What about the ...?; The last thing to talk about is a ...
> 3 Don't you think?; What do you think about that?
> 4 It's the same for me.; You're right.; I agree, although I think ...; That's true.

4 Give students three minutes working in pairs to think of different words and phrases.

> **Suggested answers**
> serious, urgent, significant, crucial, vital, essential, a necessity

5 🎧 22 Ask students to listen again and write down the words and phrases in the recording used for *important*. They can tick the ones they have already written.

> **Answers**
> Computers are also **crucial** for most people at work.
> (A fridge) is not so **essential**.
> (Fridges) are **vital** in very hot countries.
> I don't think bicycles are **a basic necessity**.
> (TV) isn't so **significant** now.

6 🎧 23 Ask students to listen to the second part of the discussion and answer the questions.

> **Answers**
> Karolina thinks the TV and the laptop and Miguel thinks the bicycle and the laptop. They don't agree on both things and it doesn't matter.

7 🎧 23 Ask students to listen again and write down what the students in the recording say. Check answers in pairs before correcting as a class.

> **Answers**
> 1 She asks Miguel: Do you want to start?
> 2 Which would you choose then?
> 3 I still think ...

Exam task

Ask students to do the task in pairs, as they would in the exam. Note the second question is slightly different from what they heard (*more important* not *less important*). Tell them they can use the words and phrases they have just written down if they want to. Remind them they have three minutes in total to do the task. Time them doing the task.

Here are some inventions that many people think are important in our daily lives.

Talk to each other about how important these things are in our daily lives.

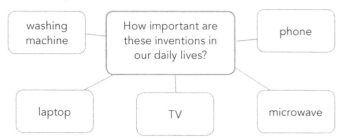

Now you have a minute to decide which two you think will become more important in the future.

Part 4

Exam task

Ask the students to answer the questions in pairs. They can say anything they like, but there are some suggested answers below.

Suggested answers

It's important in many subjects, and we use computers a lot. It's essential for science and media classes.
I like watching television occasionally. I particularly like films and comedy programmes.
No, definitely not. We communicate with technology, on our computers and mobile phones. It's just a different way of doing it.
It's not a bad thing that people are very dependent on mobile phones. I can't really imagine a world without them.
I think parents need to be careful what young children watch on TV, but some television is fun for them, and they can also learn a lot from it.

Listening

Part 1

1 Draw students' attention to the Exam tip, and tell them it is useful to identify the situation in each of the Part 1 questions and understand what they are being asked to do.

Ask them to do Exercise 1 in pairs, before they do the Exam task. Remind them that in Part 1, each of the questions is about a different situation.

Answers

1 C 2 E 3 H 4 F 5 B 6 G 7 A 8 D

Exam task

🎧 24 Ask students to do the Exam task on their own, then compare answers with a partner before you check them as a class. Play the recording twice.

You could finish by copying the script (pages 83–84) so that students can check on any answers they got wrong, or alternatively by playing again any questions that students found difficult.

Answers

1 B 2 C 3 A 4 B 5 A 6 B 7 C 8 B

Recording script

You will hear people talking in eight different situations. For questions 1–8, choose the best answer, A, B or C.

Question One. You hear a brother and sister talking.

Boy: Hey sis, I've lost everything I wrote yesterday and I've no idea why. Fortunately I backed it up on my memory stick, so I won't have to start again. Have you had any trouble with the laptop today?

Girl: Well, I know it's getting old, but it hasn't crashed on me or anything. I've been using it this morning and it seems OK. Hang on, is your project called 'Magnetism'?

Boy: Yeah …

Girl: Well, it's here, look, in my documents. You must have forgotten to switch user …

Boy: OK.

Girl: The Internet's slow though – I lost the connection once. I don't think broadband is very fast here in the village …

Question Two. You hear a sports programme on the radio.

Presenter: … and with another of the season's big races coming up tomorrow, conditions could be interesting … temperatures are set to fall rapidly overnight, with some mist forming. That may not clear completely by the time the race starts and that will mean some frost, so the track could be slippery. There were a few incidents during the last race today, with cars skidding and bumping into each other, so let's hope we don't get a repeat. Things will improve the day after, when sunny intervals and showers are predicted, so it will mean muddy conditions on the rugby field again at the weekend …

Question Three. You hear a teacher talking to his class.

Teacher: Well, I'm glad you've sorted out that little problem of leaving litter on the sports field, and just in time because we're holding a major hockey competition here on Saturday for all the schools in the area. We'd appreciate some help with that. We need about 20 volunteers, some in the car park to show where parents can drop players off, some indoors making sure everyone knows where the changing rooms are, and a few more to assist with refreshments half-way through the competition. I'll pass a list round. Put a tick against your name if you're willing to help …

Question Four. You hear a boy and girl talking about school.

Boy: You know I've always hated maths, Lucy, but I've done much better since we've had that new teacher. He makes it all seem logical …

Girl: Mmm, for me maths is relaxing – it's all there on the page. I don't enjoy the classes with the new teacher though. Although he is really good at explaining, he goes too far and makes it all a bit too simple. I'm not being pushed hard at all, you know, asked to do really difficult things in algebra and geometry and so on.

Boy: Well, yeah. If the class is right for me, it's not going to be right for you, is it?

Girl: I don't know about that …

Question Five. You hear a boy talking to his sister about a shopping trip.

Girl: How was the shopping trip, then?

Boy: The new computer store is great. You can't get near any of the play stations and stuff because there are so many people, but they sell some great games.

Girl: Where else did you go?

Boy: That fast food place. I lost Joe and Mike on the way there. I thought they were just playing a trick on me when they didn't reply to my texts. So I hid behind one of the little trees outside the fast food place and gave them a real shock when they walked past! I wish I hadn't done it now; they were upset because they couldn't find me.

Girl: Oh, are you still speaking?

Boy: Just about …

Question Six. You hear a girl talking to her class about her visit to an aquarium.

Girl: Well, yeah, I thought this visit was cool. I've done so many school trips to museums and there's only so many glass cases you can look at, even if you're interested in history! The exhibits here were alive. You walked through the glass tunnels in the aquarium and you could see the fish swimming just above your head. And then there was a place where you could actually touch some weird flat fish called rays, which really made the visit for me. Everyone should have a go at that if they can. There was a café which had an exhibition of lovely paintings and photos, too. They looked like the real thing I'd just seen.

Question Seven. You hear a boy talking about a cookery competition he entered.

Boy: … my catering teacher encouraged me to enter a baking competition, and I decided to make a cheesecake. You need lots of ingredients: biscuits and butter for the base, soft cheese, eggs, vanilla, sugar and cream for the filling and fresh raspberries and lemon for the sauce. I knew it was important not to forget anything. I could have played safe and made something very straightforward, but I wanted to make something that would impress. I was nervous – there were lots of competitors – and I forgot to put the cream into the filling. The cheesecake was great though – very firm. And the judges loved it – I came second. Result!

Question Eight. You hear a father and daughter talking about a holiday.

Girl: The holiday centre in Holland sounds great, Dad, but why are we hiring bikes?

Father: Well, the idea is that once you've arrived and put your luggage into the cabins, you park your vehicle and leave it. I think it's a good system but I'm wondering about getting the train there once we've taken the ferry to Holland. There's a station near the holiday centre. And actually there's a direct coach … we could take that from the port …

Girl: Yeah, Dad, but we'll want to get out and about, won't we? Not spend all our time in the centre …

Father: Yep, you're right. We'll stick to my original idea.

Girl: Good.

Revision key

Units 1 and 2

1 **1** arrive   **2** 're camping   **3** don't understand
4 'll be sitting   **5** don't recognise   **6** 'm doing
7 hear   **8** come

2 **1** are not / aren't as / so wide as
2 far more noise
3 is much longer than / takes much more time than
4 like best is not / isn't far
5 less often than

3 **1** C   **2** B   **3** D   **4** A   **5** B   **6** C   **7** A   **8** D

4 **1** will be   **2** I arrive   **3** arrives   **4** I think   **5** it will take
6 I've done   **7** I'll come   **8** I'm looking forward
9 I know   **10** I'm staying   **11** like   **12** will be
13 I've never seen   **14** Is there   **15** you live

5 **1** d – was playing   **2** f – had already gone
3 h – came   **4** b – haven't / have not managed
5 a – didn't answer / did not answer
6 g – haven't / have not eaten   **7** c – phoned   **8** e – had seen

6 **1** goes   **2** 're / are   **3** 'll / will be / 'm / am going to be
4 'll / will let   **5** invited   **6** had never sailed   **7** set
8 was shining   **9** 've / have been having OR 've / have had
10 knew

7 **1** excitedly   **2** definitely   **3** easily   **4** immediately
5 usually   **6** carefully   **7** simply   **8** particularly

8 **1** mysterious   **2** suitable   **3** adventurous   **4** reliable
5 natural   **6** furious   **7** predictable   **8** central

Units 3 and 4

1 **1** While   **2** Although   **3** Even though   **4** Although
5 In spite of   **6** Even though   **7** Despite   **8** Although

2 **1** was cancelled   **2** am being sent   **3** has been played by
4 had been advised (by my teacher)   **5** will be taken
6 is being made   **7** were borrowed   **8** is being put

3 **1** sound technician   **2** stuntman/woman   **3** make-up artist
4 producer   **5** cameraman/woman   **6** director
7 costume designer   **8** set decorator

4 **1** science fiction   **2** comedy   **3** thriller   **4** documentary
5 western   **6** cartoon   **7** animation   **8** horror
9 action film   **10** romantic comedy

5 **1** three of violin, cello, piano, guitar   **2** three of clarinet,
saxophone, flute, oboe   **3** five of pop, heavy metal, classical,
punk, salsa, hip-hop, rock and roll, jazz, rap, soul   **4** band
5 lyrics   **6** tune   **7** album   **8** fans

6 **1** B   **2** A   **3** B   **4** C   **5** B   **6** A   **7** C   **8** B

7 **1** of   **2** for   **3** to   **4** in   **5** on   **6** about   **7** with
8 about   **9** of   **10** about

8 **1** pitch   **2** referee   **3** goalkeeper's   **4** defenders   **5** tackle
6 umpire   **7** serve   **8** opponent   **9** point   **10** net

9 **1** convenience   **2** equality   **3** generous   **4** independence
5 patient   **6** conclusion   **7** connection   **8** divide
9 expansion   **10** persuade

Units 5 and 6

1 1 i – had been   2 g – would have missed   3 e – is
   4 j – need   5 b – help   6 h – sets   7 c – go
   8 d – would be   9 a – started   10 f – don't / do not get

2 1 secondary   2 majority   3 examination   4 comprehensive
   5 ability   6 challenging   7 variety   8 possibility
   9 choice   10 application(s)

3 1 a   2 –   3 –   4 the   5 the   6 –   7 the   8 –   9 The
   10 a   11 the   12 – / the   13 –   14 the   15 – / the   16 the
   17 a   18 –   19 the   20 an

4 1 such beautiful roses   2 so exciting   3 such good memories
   4 so good   5 such a marvellous evening   6 such a tasty
   risotto   7 so important   8 such a good laugh   9 so beautiful
   as   10 such a perfect volleyball team

5 1 air conditioning   2 electrical equipment
   3 email attachment   4 fresh ingredients   5 local produce
   6 plastic bags   7 ready meals   8 recycled paper
   9 reduce waste   10 take a shower

6 1 reduce waste   2 take a shower   3 electrical equipment
   4 recycled paper   5 email attachment   6 air conditioning
   7 plastic bags   8 local produce   9 fresh ingredients
   10 ready meals

7 1 sympathetic   2 competitive   3 decisive   4 communicative
   5 creative   6 determined   7 cheerful   8 energetic

8 1 would rather   2 is looking forward   3 would like
   4 can't imagine   5 would prefer   6 dislike
   7 have never been able   8 suggested

Units 7 and 8

1 1 to go   2 to fall   3 to do   4 taking   5 swimming
   6 relaxing   7 driving   8 to find   9 putting   10 go
   11 looking   12 to go

2 1 explained (that) he couldn't
   2 agreed to help / agreed (that) she would help
   3 so I can't come
   4 hadn't seen such a
   5 told me she liked
   6 if I knew

3 1 dress   2 suit   3 make   4 get   5 look   6 keep   7 show
   8 go   9 come   10 try   11 have   12 get

4 1 passionate   2 frustrated   3 optimistic   4 curious
   5 guilty   6 patient

5 ashamed – 5   confident – 3   enthusiastic – 1   furious – 2
   interested – 4   irritated – 2

6 1 who   2 whose   3 which / that   4 who / that   5 where
   6 where   7 which   8 which / that / –

7 1 recycling   2 disease   3 endangered   4 cell
   5 conservation   6 genetics   7 atom   8 electricity

8 1 strength   2 powerful   3 originally   4 possibilities
   5 impolite   6 attractive   7 commercials
   8 misunderstanding

Writing guide key

Essay

1 **1** your English teacher **2** yes **3** no, it's not necessary
4 yes

2 Paragraphs 1, 2 and 4 discuss point 1, which subjects are
most useful. Paragraph 3 talks about point 2, which subjects
are easier. The candidate says that science subjects are only
useful for certain jobs, whereas languages are useful for
everyone, and that science subjects are very difficult for
many people.

The candidate's third point (in paragraph three) is that
people should study both science and languages if possible.

The conclusion is that everyone should study foreign
languages.

Plan

Paragraph 1: 'which is more useful' depends on what job
you are doing; science isn't useful for everyone

Paragraph 2: learning different languages is useful for
everyone

Paragraph 3: good to study both sciences and languages if
possible, but science more difficult

Paragraph 4: everyone should study languages

Linking phrases

I would like to start my essay by saying that whether
languages or sciences are more useful depends very
much on what job you would like to do. If you want to
be a doctor, or a great inventor, of course you will need
to study science subjects. However, I would argue
that there really isn't much point in studying science
subjects if you are going to be a history teacher, or
work in a shop.

On the other hand, learning languages is always
useful, whatever career you want to have in the future.
Of course, English is very useful because so many
people speak it, but other languages, like Spanish and
Chinese, are also very important.

I think that it is good to study both sciences and
languages if you can, but not many people will become
experts in science. That is because for most people,
science beyond a certain level is far too difficult,
although it's good to have a basic knowledge.

Therefore, I would like to conclude by saying
that, ideally, everyone should study several foreign
languages, simply because they are useful in every job.

Story

1 **1** teacher/other students who read the school website

2 a day

3 The events don't have to be positive. They weren't
planned. The story begins 'I was expecting to have a
quiet day, but it turned out to be just the opposite'.

2 The first point is in the second paragraph: 'George told me
there was a robbery going on.'

The second point is in the first paragraph: '... when the
phone rang'

Past tenses

Past simple throughout e.g.: *turned out, was, asked,
rushed, told, said, phoned, arrived, took, were, appeared*

Past continuous: *was expecting, was reading, were being
removed* (passive)

Past perfect: *had driven up, had stopped*

Past perfect continuous: *had been moving*

Direct speech

It is used by the candidate/narrator to his friend George. It
adds excitement and tension to the story, and shows how
the boys are feeling.

Effective vocabulary and expressions

The following are included: *reading sleepily, there's a
much simpler explanation, said impatiently, arrived very
rapidly, our picture appeared in the paper*

Title

This sets the scene for the story and makes you want to
read on. The candidate has clearly planned what he is going
to write about. So always give your story a title!

Review

1 **1** other teenagers

2 in a magazine

3 Any kind – as long as you really like it yourself.

4 You don't have to recommend it – the question says
'*whether* you would recommend it to other people'.
However, if it's your favourite website, and you spend
a lot of time on it, you will probably recommend it to
someone!

2 Linking words and phrases

My favourite website

The best website I have been on is ultimateguitar.com.
I spend lots of time on it <u>because</u> I'm learning to play
the electric guitar and everything I need is on this site.

It has reviews of all kinds of guitar music, <u>which
means</u> jazz and classical <u>as well</u> as pop, rock and <u>so</u>
on, so there is something for different tastes. <u>In
addition</u>, there is always news and gossip about well-
known guitarists. <u>And better still</u>, there are really
good interviews to watch with rock stars, classical
guitarists and so on.

<u>However</u>, the most fantastic thing about the site is
that you can download tabs for all your favourite guitar
music from it. It has all the famous riffs and they add
new music every week. <u>It's such</u> a popular feature <u>that</u>
there is sometimes a queue for downloading. I set it up
before school, <u>so</u> it's there when I get home.

I love this website, and I would recommend it to other
guitar fans, <u>especially</u> if they are players themselves.
And <u>even if you don't</u> play, I'm sure you will find it
interesting!

Verb tenses

The main tense used is the present simple. Other tenses
include the present perfect: *have been*; the present
continuous: *I'm learning*; the future: *you will find*

Vocabulary

Words related to websites: *site, to go on a website,
download, tabs*

Words related to music: *electric guitar, jazz, classical, pop,
rock, rock stars, (classical) guitarist, riffs, players*

Letter and email

1 1 your English friend Hannah

   2 yes, any capital city

   3 Yes, you're asked to recommend something for a tourist
      to visit – that could be anything, including cafés, shops, a
      funfair, a sports stadium, etc.

2 Historical facts: *Romans, French kings, Baron Haussmann,
   French Revolution*

   Places to visit: *The Louvre, the Latin Quarter, River Seine*

   Friendly phrases: *Your history project sounds fascinating!,
   Best wishes*

3 Thanking, Stating opinion or preference, Suggesting and
   recommending, Giving reasons, Apologising, Making
   requests and offers, Asking questions.

Article

1 1 in a teenage magazine

   2 teenagers of different nationalities

   3 No, you don't have to use the suggestions, but you can if
      you wish.

2 **Plan**

   Paragraph 1: Moon always important / beauty

   Paragraph 2: Space travel / living on the moon / science
   fiction

   Paragraph 3: Children's stories / songs / poems

Set text

1 **Miss Havisham**

   Her appearance: still dressed for her wedding; her dress has
   turned yellow

   Her behaviour: she stopped all the clocks in the house
   and lives in the past; she brought Estelle up to dislike men
   because of what happened to her.

   Reason why she is strange: She is strange because her
   future husband stood her up on her wedding day, and she
   has never got over the shock.

2 **Phantom of the Opera**
   Plan

   Paragraph 1: explain who phantom was – Erik, a man with
   an ugly face who lived in the Opera house, a real person,
   not a ghost, loved Christine

   Paragraph 2: sad life, poor, made to wear a mask

   Paragraph 3: Erik travelled, was brilliant, built Opera house
   for Christine

   Relevant parts of the plot

   Normal person, not a ghost, built Opera House, taught
   Christine to sing and fell in love with her, born in a poor
   village, made to wear a mask

Workbook key and recording scripts

Unit 1

Listening Part 3

Exam task

1 E 2 D 3 B 4 H 5 F

Recording script

You will hear five short extracts in which people are talking about their best friend. For questions 1–5, choose from the list A–H what each speaker particularly likes about their friend. Use the letters only once. There are three extra letters which you do not need to use. Play the recording twice.

You now have 30 seconds to look at Part Three.

Speaker 1

Well, I'm really lucky because I've known my best friend since we were at primary school together. I think one of the reasons we get on so well is that we are both a bit quiet. For example, we can sit in silence on a long journey together and feel quite comfortable. I think the most important thing though is that we're definitely similar in our likes and dislikes. We're both into the same films, and dress in similar styles and colours. That means a lot to both of us. Oh, and we both laugh a lot too, although not at the same things!

Speaker 2

I get kind of mad quite often at the moment, and I think that's difficult for most people! My brother and I have certainly fallen out big time. So, really, Bob is special because he doesn't take any notice of my moods. He just sort of puts up with them. And best of all he's always on my side. He usually has no idea why I'm angry, but that's okay with him. He's nearly always happy so he's a good person to have around. We're comfortable with each other, we enjoy each other's company and we talk for hours.

Speaker 3

There aren't many people I've known as long as Sarah. We've been friends for years. We went to each other's birthday parties when we were little, and we know each other's families really well. There are lots of things we can remember doing together, and that's extremely important to our friendship. We're sort of like sisters in some ways, but we don't argue – which is just as well because Sarah would always win – she's a much stronger personality than me! We're actually very different, and we have very different tastes in most things. It means there's always loads to talk about.

Speaker 4

Well, Jim's been my best mate since we started at secondary school four years ago. We do a lot of sport together and have fun. We're in the same football team. We get on because he knows what affects me, you know, why I react as I do to stuff. He's similar to me in that way, I guess. That's what's really good about having him as a friend. We both get really cross when we don't win something – we're very competitive. We're in the same class next year – we've both chosen science subjects so it'll be good to do some studying together too.

Speaker 5

My friend Annie's fun to be around, always laughing and cheerful. She loves animals, and wants to be a vet. We work together in science at school and she's so much better at it than me and is really good at remembering all the formulas and stuff, but she doesn't seem to mind when I mess something up – a project or an experiment – and it's the same outside school too. I really appreciate that. Annie loves riding and she's persuaded me to give it a try. We're going on Saturday, and I have to say I'm a bit nervous, but I expect I'll be all right!

Grammar

1 1 in 2 in 3 every 4 at 5 in 6 on 7 – 8 in 9 all 10 at

2 1 than 2 great / good 3 as / so 4 to 5 much / far 6 less 7 as 8 more 9 the 10 less

Reading and Use of English Part 5

1 1 brother and sister 2 cakes in a shop window 3 Because his sister has just told him that she made some of the cakes in the window.

Exam task

2 1 C 2 B 3 A

Vocabulary

1 1 A produce B involve C play D make

2 A get B increase C change D happen

3 A total B amount C size D number

4 A highly B hugely C deeply D particularly

2 1 hit it off 2 takes after 3 get on well with 4 fell out with 5 have / 've been going out together 6 socialise 7 have / 've got to know 8 fell for

Reading and Use of English Part 1

Exam task

1 B 2 D 3 A 4 D 5 C 6 A 7 B 8 C

Unit 2

Reading and Use of English Part 6

1 1 yes 2 yes

2 1 B 2 C 3 A 4 C

Listening Part 1

Exam task

1 B 2 C 3 C 4 A 5 C 6 C 7 A 8 B

1 Wednesday is likely to be a very wet day

2 ... there was so much variety too, you know, pop songs in with the classical stuff ...

Yes, no way I was expecting that.

3 as soon as I said I'd like a bit of guidance on my project, she told me exactly what I needed to know

4 he did something to his ankle, didn't he? He had to come off the pitch

5 I can see now though that I'll have to put in a lot of effort if I'm going to get anywhere – even more than I thought

6 there were complaints as some cyclists rode through the villages at tremendous speed paying no attention to residents.

7 my dad just rang to say he'll pick me up at your house afterwards instead of in town

8 you're always trying out different things

Recording script

You will hear people talking in eight different situations. For questions 1–8, choose the best answer (A, B or C). Play the recording twice.

1

You hear a teacher talking to her class about a camping trip.

Well, I know you're all looking forward to the trip, but several of you have said you're worried about camping in the cold. The good news is that it looks as though we've seen the last of freezing nights and icy mornings, so relax. Apparently, <u>Wednesday is likely to be a very wet day</u>, so we'll do our museum visit then, but that's it, there's no chance of stormy weather where we're going, though they might get some here while we're away. So let's hope the forecast is right, and see you at eight o'clock on Monday morning!

2

You hear two friends talking about a concert.

Girl: Great concert! That first violinist was just fabulous to watch ...

Boy: I thought he would be ... I saw him on TV the other day ... he's dead cool.

Girl: Yeah, I wish I could play the violin like that. There was <u>so much variety too, you know pop songs in with the classical stuff.</u>

Boy: <u>Yes, no way I was expecting that!</u>

Girl: Me neither. And I loved the concert hall, really modern, looked a bit like a spaceship. I thought concert halls were all dark wood and red seats.

Boy: Some of them are. Not that one though. There was an article about it in the local paper the other day. My mum showed it to me.

Girl: Right ...

3

You hear a girl talking to her brother.

Boy: Did you get to see Mrs Kirby then? Did she tell you what you'd missed in the last lesson?

Girl: Yes, and as soon as <u>I said I'd like a bit of guidance on my project</u>, she told me exactly what I needed to know and I wrote it all down. She offered me some notes on how to write the introduction and conclusion but I don't need them. I know what I'm doing now. She didn't even tell me off for not giving the work in yet. So I'll finish it tonight and give it to her in the morning.

Boy: She sounds really reasonable ...

Girl: Yeah, she's great, and you'll probably get her for history next year, too.

Boy: Cool.

4

You hear two friends discussing a rugby match they watched.

Boy 1: Did you see the France–Wales match on TV last night? Exciting stuff – and Wales won! No wonder all those fans rushed onto the pitch when the match had finished. Everyone was over the moon!

Boy 2: Yeah, I was too. I watched it with my dad. What happened to Gareth Jones though – did the referee decide he was in the wrong over that tackle?

Boy 1: Nah, it was OK but <u>he did something to his ankle,</u> didn't he? He had to come off the pitch. Don't think it's serious though ... he's in the team for next Saturday.

Boy 2: Great, I'll be watching that too ... want to come round to my place and watch it with me?

5

You hear a boy telling a girl about a lesson he has just had.

Girl: What was your first Russian lesson like, Joe?

Boy: Well, the teacher spoke only Russian for the first half an hour but we learnt to say our names and a few other things!

Girl: I didn't choose Russian as I thought it might be hard with the different alphabet.

Boy: Yeah – it isn't as easy for us as some other languages. I was going to do Spanish but I like a challenge so this is good for me. <u>I can see now though that I'll have to put in a lot of effort if I'm going to get anywhere</u> – even more than I thought – but I'm OK with that.

6

You hear a news report about a cycle ride.

The annual 50 kilometre cycle ride around Middleton took place today. 10,000 cyclists had registered. That's the maximum so people who turned up on the day couldn't join in unfortunately. We'd had a lot of rain and there was a worry that some of the roads might be muddy but it was all OK in the end. There's a prize for the fastest time and there were complaints as <u>some cyclists rode through the villages at tremendous speed paying no attention to residents. That's not in the spirit of the day</u> which is a community event for everyone to enjoy. And for the most part everyone did just that!

7

You hear a girl leaving a message on an answerphone.

Hi, Louisa. I'm on my way. I'll be there in about 20 minutes. I've just had my music lesson. I'm a bit later than I said as I stayed behind to have a chat with my teacher – she's really nice. I'm just walking to your place and then we'll catch the bus together to the cinema. We'll have to get the bus back too because <u>my dad just rang to say he'll pick me up at your house afterwards instead of in town as he's got to work late now.</u> I bumped into Jamie this morning who was with a few friends and he said he might come so I told him what time.

8

You hear two friends talking about surfing.

Girl:	Hi, Ben. Have you been surfing again?
Boy:	Yeah, I love it. I know you've never tried, Anna, but you should.
Girl:	Not sure – I'm not a very good swimmer.
Boy:	Good enough. You're so sporty – <u>you're always trying out different things.</u> Surfing would be another one to add to your list. You could be really good at it and I could show you what to do. And I know the best places to go – there are loads round here.
Girl:	But I'm not very competitive.
Boy:	It's not about that so much – you get to know the other people and that makes you try harder when you watch them – but it's more about your own satisfaction.

Grammar

1 1 C

2 C

3 We used to live in the city centre, but we live in the country now.

4 C

5 C

6 John used to be able to play the guitar well, but he's forgotten everything now.

7 C

8 I didn't use to / didn't like ice cream when I was young because it was too cold.

2 1 for 2 since 3 ago 4 for 5 ago 6 Since
7 since 8 for

Vocabulary

1 **Across: 4** relaxing **5** disappointing **9** thrilling
11 embarrassed **13** astonished **14** exhausting

Down: 1 fascinated **2** disappointed **3** fascinating
6 thrilled **7** impressed **8** astonishing **10** relaxed
12 worried

2 1 criticism 2 championship 3 darkness 4 fitness
5 friendship 6 happiness 7 illness 8 journalism
9 laziness 10 membership 11 relationship 12 weakness

3 1 careful / careless 2 childish / childless 3 foolish
4 harmful / harmless 5 predictable 6 priceless
7 profitable 8 selfish / selfless 9 stylish
10 usable / useful / useless

4 1 adj – predictable 2 n – criticism 3 adj – selfish
4 n – laziness 5 n – championship 6 adj – useless
7 adj – priceless 8 adj – childish 9 n – fitness
10 n – membership

Reading and Use of English Part 3

Exam task

1 freedom 2 tourism 3 originally 4 height
5 inexperienced 6 responsibility 7 carelessness
8 frightening

Unit 3

Listening Part 4

1 1 B 2 D 3 A 4 C

2 1 ✓ 2 ✓ 3 ✓ 4 ✗ 5 ✗ 6 ✓ 7 ✗

Exam task

1 C 2 B 3 C 4 B 5 A 6 A 7 C

Recording script

You will hear an interview with Jasmine Chang, who is studying at circus school. For questions 1–7, choose the best answer (A, B or C). Play the recording twice.

You now have one minute to look at Part Four.

Interviewer:	And today we have Jasmine Chang in the studio, who's going to talk about circus school and working for a circus. Welcome Jasmine.
Jasmine:	Thanks.
Int:	So Jasmine, what does a day at circus school consist of?
Jasmine:	Well, in some ways it's just like regular school – (1) <u>my days are packed with classes</u>. Not only physical stuff like acrobatics, movement and ballet, but also theatre, music and circus history. We have classes from nine till four, and then there's extra time for individual training. It's really full on. You have to be keen to keep up with it all.
Int:	And what made you decide to go to circus school?
Jasmine:	Well, ever since I was a little girl I've loved everything about the circus. My family could never really understand it. At first it was the bright lights and the clothes. (2) <u>Then I realised that because I was good at gymnastics, if I studied I could become a circus star myself.</u> And what I like is that circus school challenges me – I learn something new every day.
Int:	And you've already performed in front of an audience, haven't you?
Jasmine:	Well ... I've done (3) <u>hundreds of acrobatics workshops with children</u>, and I've been to lots of events. That's included everything from helping to make clown costumes at a summer festival to giving a talk with a friend about how to be a trapeze performer! And to be honest, I've enjoyed them all.
Int:	But it must take such a lot of effort for a show to run smoothly and to get everything to a high standard.

Jasmine:	Well, if you're doing acrobatics of any kind like me, you obviously need to be very flexible. For trapeze, you need a lot of upper body strength to keep yourself swinging backwards and forwards. That's not so important for all the performers, like clowns for instance. For the audience, it should all look as though we're hardly trying – that it's effortless. But to achieve that, (4) what every circus act needs is months of practice so that the performers are almost doing everything automatically and smoothly even though it's often quite dangerous.
Int:	Are there any interesting jobs for people to do behind the scenes at the circus?
Jasmine:	Oh yeah, if you don't think you have what it takes to be constantly performing on stage, there are lots of jobs like designing scenery that don't require physical activity. You can also work backstage with the costumes and helping the performers with their make-up. And the big circus companies take on people with technical skills, (5) working with the microphones and lights. That's the really interesting and creative work, definitely something to go for if you can.
Int:	OK, and after you've trained at circus school, how do you find a job?
Jasmine:	It depends. There are circus performers that don't work for a single circus, but instead (6) try to get a part in a particular show, like an actor does for different movies. That's hard in some ways, as you might not always be in work, but it's a good way to get going in a career, so I think it's the best option. It's hard to get a permanent job in a circus, and I've been told you need to be able to perform at a very high standard all the time if you want to keep your job, so there's a lot of pressure.
Int:	Is circus work particularly dangerous for performers?
Jasmine:	Well, it can be if you don't warm up properly and stretch so you don't hurt yourself. But to be honest, that's the same for lots of professions isn't it, like ballet, for example? (7) You take risks in all the jobs where you are on a stage. But circus is such fun. And, as with any job, if you've done all the proper training you should be fine.
Int:	It's been great talking to you, Jasmine.
Jasmine:	Thank you.

Vocabulary

1 musicians   2 composer   3 guitarist   4 recording
5 rehearsal   6 traditional   7 classical   8 conductor

Reading and Use of English Part 7

1 1 J   2 E   3 I   4 D   5 G   6 B   7 F   8 L   9 A   10 C
2 1 B   2 A   3 B   4 B   5 A   6 B   7 A   8 A

Vocabulary

1 screens   2 chat   3 celebrities   4 presenter   5 comedian
6 role   7 documentary   8 channel   9 soap   10 character

Grammar

1 1 but   2 Despite   3 in spite of   4 however   5 despite
   6 although   7 In spite of   8 but
2 1 will be included   2 Is ... being filmed   3 has been done
   4 wasn't given   5 was being rehearsed   6 have been made
   7 was being played   8 have been given
3 1 having, cleaned   2 had, cut   3 having / going to have,
   painted   4 had, stolen   5 have, tested   6 had, corrected
   7 have had, installed   8 had, taken

Reading and Use of English Part 4

1 had my bike fixed   2 although it had rained   3 had not /
hadn't seen for   4 nobody had told me   5 is the least popular
of / among   6 was frightened by

Unit 4

Reading and Use of English Part 5

1 1 suspicious   2 embarrassed   3 disappointed   4 astonished
   5 discouraged   6 jealous
2 He felt disappointed.
3 D
4 B

Vocabulary

1 beat the record, energy levels, football pitch, ice rink,
   play rugby, score a goal, tennis court, win the cup
2 1 football pitch   2 beat the record   3 playing rugby
   4 scoring a goal   5 energy levels   6 an ice rink
   7 won the cup   8 tennis court

Listening Part 2

1 stick 2 goalie 3 skates 4 ice 5 puck 6 net

Exam task

1 speed 2 specialised 3 reaction 4 tiring 5 fitness
6 stick 7 helmet 8 ability 9 July 10 confidence

Recording script

You will hear a teenager called Sam Lloyd talking to his class about ice hockey. For questions 1–10, complete the sentences with a word or short phrase. Play the recording twice.

You now have 45 seconds to look at Part Two.

Well, I'm going to talk to you today about a sport I've just taken up – ice hockey. It's actually one of the most popular games in the world. You hear a lot about it, because it needs so much skill and it's a great spectator sport. It's exciting stuff, too. Some of it's really acrobatic, especially for the guy in goal! (1) <u>What appeals to me though is the speed that it's played at</u>. For me, that's what's always made it thrilling, and what made me want to play myself. So, for those of you who don't know much about the game, ice hockey matches are played on a rink, and there are six players on each team. That's three players on attack, two in defence and a goalie – that's what you call the goalkeeper – in front of the net. One of the interesting things about ice hockey is that (2) <u>goalies are really specialised players</u>. They never play in the other positions. Other players do, although they almost never play in goal.

Another thing that sets it apart from other team sports is that in ice hockey, every movement of players on the opposing team (3) <u>needs a reaction from every member of your team</u>. As there are only six players on each side, everyone has to be aware of and involved in what's going on all over the rink all the time. Now the puck – that's the rubber disc they use like a ball – goes at 90 mph, so it's busy!

You need to concentrate all the time, and that means (4) <u>it's really tiring for the players</u>. I think that's why each game consists of three periods of 20 minutes each, and the players get 15 minutes rest between them. You need time to recover!

Last season, when I started playing, I did an eight-week course for beginners at the club here in the city. It was a great way to start because (5) <u>it included basic fitness</u> and balance. Now that was really useful, as you don't want to spend your whole time falling over!

Once I'd done the basics and got the hang of the skating skills, I moved on to some special coaching sessions they did. Those were on (6) <u>stick skills</u> for ice hockey, which are very important. I thought it was good that they let you learn at your own pace, you could just ask for help and advice when you wanted it. I was dead keen, so I just kept asking!

I bought some kit of my own right away – (7) <u>the minimum you need is gloves, helmet and skates</u>. You can borrow the rest of the kit all the time you're a junior, the club has loan kit, but people buy their own protective clothing as soon as they get into a proper team. You can buy second-hand stuff, so it's not too expensive.

I've started to play in the games for juniors that the coaches organise at the club now. (8) <u>They always try and ensure the players are matched for ability</u>. That means they're probably the same age too. It makes the game more enjoyable and means people are less likely to injure themselves. I've been okay so far, just a few bruises!

I did my first hockey course in the summer holidays. The hockey season is basically October until April, so (9) <u>I'd say that July is a good time of year to get started</u> if you want to get involved quickly in the sport.

And I think if you do take up ice hockey, you'll really love it, and you'll learn a lot. (10) <u>I've got much more confidence now</u> than I used to have. I guess ice hockey's like other sports in that respect, you get much more from it than general fitness and learning how to play ...

So, if you're interested, go for it!

Vocabulary

1 do, make

   do: your best, a course, your duty, homework, housework, research, sport

   make: arrangements, changes, a decision, an effort, friends, a good impression, a mistake, a noise, a success of, a suggestion

2 1 make, decision   2 made, good impression   3 do, homework
   4 make, suggestion   5 made, mistake   6 do, duty
   7 made, success   8 do, best   9 made, arrangements
   10 make, effort

Grammar

1 1 There's   2 there's going to be / will be / may be / might be
   3 It's / It would be   4 Is there / Is there going to be / Will there
   be   5 is it   6 There hasn't been   7 Will there be / Is there
   8 Will it be   9 It isn't / wasn't   10 There was / used to be

2 1 from   2 about   3 in   4 to   5 in   6 on   7 in   8 on
   9 at   10 on

3 1 must / have to / need to remember to   2 don't need
   3 haven't been able   4 can't be Peter's   5 should have phoned
   6 must be   7 might have fallen   8 was able to

4 1 might   2 can   3 should   4 must   5 shouldn't   6 can't

Reading and Use of English Part 2

1 Apart   2 order   3 instead   4 as   5 up   6 or   7 such   8 mine

Exam task

1 were   2 than   3 up   4 which   5 After   6 as   7 one   8 well

Unit 5

Listening Part 2

Exam task

1 personality 2 hairdresser 3 police 4 priorities
5 promotion 6 qualifications 7 chemist 8 money 9 chef
10 experience

> **Recording script**
>
> *You will hear a teacher at a secondary school giving some students advice about how to choose a career. For questions 1–10, complete the sentences with a word or short phrase. Play the recording twice. You now have 45 seconds to look at Part Two.*
>
> Good morning everyone. As you know I'm here to talk to you as you start to make decisions about what careers you want to do in future. It's an exciting thing to be thinking about, and it's important to get it right. (1) <u>You need to choose something which will match your skills, of course, but also something that you feel works for your personality</u> as well. And the good news is that there are just so many interesting and rewarding jobs to choose from these days.
>
> So, where do you begin? Well, it's important to choose a career that you're going to be successful in, so you need to be realistic about what you're good at. So for instance, (2) <u>someone who likes meeting people and talking to them might enjoy being a hairdresser</u>, but hate working as a technician, which is a job that's behind the scenes and doesn't involve much contact with people. And if you're good at handling difficult situations and (3) <u>finding a solution after an argument, you might like to sign up with the police</u>. You probably wouldn't be happy working for a company in an office job where there wasn't much challenge.
>
> After that, the next step is to decide what you want from a job, so it's a good idea to sit down and make a list. (4) <u>Write down your priorities</u>. There are several things to consider. For example, do you want a job which gives you satisfaction and makes you feel that you've done something worthwhile at the end of the day? Alternatively, is (5) <u>it important that you'll get promotion after a few years</u>? These are things you really have to consider before you make any decisions.
>
> Now, when you've reached that stage, and decided that a particular job might be for you, (6) <u>you should find out if there are any qualifications</u> that you need. Do you have to have a degree to do the job, or will they accept you for training without one? Knowing that might affect decisions about what you do here at school.
>
> Moving on, another factor to consider is where the jobs you'd like to do are located. If you want to become a teacher or a nurse, there are jobs all over the country, but (7) <u>if you want to be a chemist, you know, and work in a pharmaceutical company, there are fewer jobs, and they may not be near where you live</u>, so you have to decide whether that will be a problem for you.
>
> Now, there's one thing I haven't mentioned so far, and that's (8) <u>money. I would say it's important to realise that it isn't the chief consideration</u> when it comes to making career choices now, although it may become increasingly important as you get older. The most important things at the moment are interest and enjoyment, and finding something you have the ability to do.
>
> And there's something else I'd like to point out. I'd definitely say that if you have a real passion for something, then see if there's a job you can do related to it. (9) <u>So if you love cooking, why not think about becoming a chef</u>? It may turn out to be just the job for you.
>
> There's one final suggestion I'd like to make. Before you make any firm decisions about a long-term career, it's very important, whatever you all decide to do, (10) <u>to try and gain some experience</u>. Any is better than none! And if you want to be a doctor or dentist, as a few of you have already mentioned, you may find that medical schools will only consider your application if you've already spent some time working as a volunteer in your local hospital.
>
> OK, I hope that's given you all a clear idea of where to start. Now, does anyone have any questions?

Reading and Use of English Part 7

1 Film: A cameraman's view, Hollywood greats

History: Ancient Egypt, A century of food

Language: Contemporary poets, Storytellers

Science: The rainforest, Sea creatures, Inside the human body, 21st-century space travel

Sport: Fun and fitness, Surf safari

2 No, they are about different camps.

Yes, they did.

Exam task

1 C 2 E 3 C 4 D 5 E 6 B 7 C 8 A 9 D 10 A

Vocabulary

1 into 2 at 3 over 4 away with 5 out of 6 round to 7 to
8 up 9 across 10 for 11 by 12 ahead 13 on 14 through
15 off

Grammar

1 1 future 2 past 3 present 4 present 5 past
6 (near) future

2 1 had finished 2 had gone 3 saw 4 lived 5 didn't talk
6 would let 7 hadn't lost 8 sat 9 weren't 10 had brought

3 1 I hadn't / had not shouted at 2 would / 'd rather you caught
3 I (can) call Sam before 4 wouldn't / would not have had to
5 hoped (that) I would get 6 in case it is / it's 7 unless my
parents agree 8 we're / we are not / we aren't / don't get
given

Reading and Use of English Part 1

Exam task

1 D 2 A 3 C 4 D 5 B 6 A 7 C 8 D

Unit 6

Listening Part 4

You will hear about: birds, the environment, famous buildings, history, plants, sport.

Exam task

1 C   2 B   3 A   4 C   5 C   6 B   7 C

> **Recording script**
>
> *You will hear an English girl called Annie talking about a trip her family made to Australia. For questions 1–7, choose the best answer (A, B or C). Play the recording twice.*
>
> *You now have one minute to look at Part Four.*
>
> Well, it was definitely the best holiday my family's ever had. We flew into Sydney, and then just chilled out for a day.
>
> Anyway, the first lunchtime, we were eating a burger in an outdoor café when four parrots landed on the next table. The waiter put some sugar out for them – like he would have done for his pets. Later that evening, some bats started flying around our heads. Everyone makes such a fuss about them here in the UK. People are scared of them. To Australians though, they're just part of the scenery, and (1) <u>I realised that they're used to having animals around. Town and country are all kind of mixed in together</u> – it's different from the UK.
>
> Then, the next morning we headed off to the Blue Mountains. It's a national park outside Sydney, where we walked for miles through the eucalyptus trees. They smell wonderful, so I didn't mind the distances that Dad made us walk! There are sandstone cliffs too – the most famous ones are called The Three Sisters. They look wonderful at sunset. (2) <u>They're lit up at night, although I thought that it wasn't really appropriate to do that in a national park</u>. I loved the waterfalls though, they're not polluted and they look and sound fantastic. We spent three days there.
>
> Then we drove on to Tobruk sheep station, which is a huge sheep farm open to the public. The stockmen who work there are like the Australian version of American cowboys. They get around the farms on horseback. (3) <u>We saw the sheepdogs working with the sheep – that was great fun</u>. They're so intelligent, they run round the sheep, over them even! We got to drink tea round a campfire, too. My dad talked to some of the older men about the history of sheep farming in Australia – it was a hard life.
>
> Anyhow, we stayed at the farm overnight. I thought it would be incredibly quiet, but you could hear all sorts of animals as night fell! You can borrow a telescope to look at the sky, too. (4) <u>There are thousands of stars out in the bush. I had no idea it would be like that because I've always lived in a town</u>. We had to get up early the next day – we'd been warned about that though. Everything starts at dawn because it's so hot at midday.
>
> The next day we headed back to Sydney, to the beach. Of course you can just picnic and do the usual stuff like swimming. We tried surfing too – there are loads of schools where you can get lessons. And I loved it. I was pretty good at standing up but when I did fall off, (5) <u>the board knocked me on the head a few times</u>. That spoilt it a bit for me, although I did manage to keep my mouth shut and avoid drinking the salt water! My brother loved surfing ... he's got good balance, he's done some skiing, and it probably helped him.
>
> And finally, we went to see some of the famous sights in the city, like the Sydney Opera House, where there was a tour that Mum and I really enjoyed, and (6) <u>the Maritime Museum</u>, which had historic ships and stuff to look around. That <u>kept us all happy for hours</u>. Of course I took tons of photos, especially when Dad and I walked across the Harbour Bridge, because the views were just amazing.
>
> So, that's it! I loved Australia. Do go if you get the chance. We want to go back. We might go to the Ningaloo Reef and go snorkelling but there are lots of other things to do which are just as exciting. You won't see the whole country in one trip, so it's best to focus on one area like we did. Australia's huge, and there are miles of empty desert. You can do trips there to see (7) <u>the cave art done by the first Australians ... go in winter</u>, when it's not so hot if you want to do that. Now, to finish ...

Vocabulary

1   1 B   2 A   3 A   4 B   5 B   6 A

2   1 keep up with   2 came out   3 turned out   4 comes out
5 turned out   6 keep up with

Grammar

1   1 Was the film <u>exciting enough</u> for you?

2 It's very late and we are <u>too</u> tired to eat.

3 We tried to light a candle but the wind was <u>too</u> strong.

4 The streets are dirty because <u>there isn't enough money</u> to clean them.

5 I think we would be <u>too</u> exhausted to enjoy the wonderful view if we cycled.

6 The month of May is best for holidays because the weather isn't <u>too hot</u>.

2   1 so   2 such   3 so   4 such   5 such   6 so

Reading and Use of English Part 2

Exam task

1 long   2 Although   3 so   4 where   5 a   6 one   7 out
8 be

Reading and Use of English Part 6

1   It started because Felix Finkbeiner gave a presentation at school about climate change, and became very interested in planting trees.

2   He has got young people in over 130 countries involved in the project and received support from Toyota.

Exam task

1 D   2 C   3 G   4 F   5 E   6 A

Grammar

1   bar of chocolate, breath of fresh air, can of soup, flash of lightning, item of clothing, means of transport, piece of advice, shower of rain, slice of cheese, tube of toothpaste

2   1 can of soup   2 tube of toothpaste   3 flash of lightning
4 breath of fresh air   5 slice of cheese   6 means of transport   7 item of clothing   8 shower of rain   9 bar of chocolate   10 piece of advice

Unit 7

Reading and Use of English Part 5

The girls are busking on the street.

Exam task

1 D   2 C   3 B   4 D   5 B   6 D

Vocabulary

Across: 1 head   3 sure   4 impression   7 humour   8 breath   9 fun   10 temper   11 ears   12 trick

Down: 2 disappointment   5 sick   6 nerves   9 fool

Listening Part 3

1 **A** horse riding   **B** climbing in the tree tops   **C** quad biking

Exam task

1 H   2 A   3 B   4 G   5 E

Recording script

You will hear five short extracts in which people are talking about outings they went on with their families. For questions 1–5, choose from the list A–H how each speaker felt about the outing. Use the letters only once. There are three extra letters which you do not need to use. Play the recording twice.

You now have 30 seconds to look at Part Three.

Speaker 1

I visited some famous botanical gardens with my family. There are glasshouses there where you can see all sorts of tropical plants. I didn't think it would be very interesting before we went because I knew there weren't any activities and I generally like doing really active things. Anyway, in the biggest glasshouse there was this amazing rainforest, complete with a waterfall. There was some information given about all the plants and I'm definitely going to make an effort to find out more ... I loved it there. It was really hot and humid by the way ...

Speaker 2

We all went to this horse-riding centre for my birthday. I'd never been on a horse before and boy was I nervous. If you've got no experience, you have a lesson first with an instructor and they put you on a very gentle horse. My horse was called Toffee, and she was very calm. I relaxed, so I got on well and was allowed to join the morning ride into the countryside. There were so many different things to do at the centre, it was great. We had a nice lunch, there were films to watch and the day finished with a little show by the experienced riders.

Speaker 3

Yeah, we all went to this climbing centre where you go right up in the tree tops. I couldn't wait to try it out. You do an instruction programme first, and you wear a safety harness all the time you're up high. You walk along these rope paths, and you can swing across and slide down a series of ropes and wires. I'd never done anything like it before and it was just fantastic to find out how to do something completely new. In the end, I didn't find it all that difficult – I would have liked to have gone higher up. My brother found it a real challenge though.

Speaker 4

I got to go quad biking. I wasn't sure if I would like it but I loved it! You spend an hour going over the basics before you go on the track. The guy who sorted us out had obviously been instructing for a while. Anyway, when we went it was wet, and we got covered in mud. It was fun though. I thought I'd find it hard at first and I did, but it was well worth it because I had a great time. There are different tracks you can go on, and then at the end of the day, you do a race.

Speaker 5

We spent a day at the sea-life centre down by the beach. There were loads of animals and fish, all kept in different pools. They also look after a lot of seals there, especially the young ones – the pups – that have been found on the beach. They need feeding, and I was actually allowed to do that. It was a bit like holding a little dog! I hadn't been expecting anything like that, and I loved it. There was loads to see – everything from seahorses to sharks. I'm not sure that I learnt very much, but it was interesting, and I took some awesome photos.

Grammar

1 *to*-infinitive: aim, arrange, decide, deserve, manage, offer, pretend, refuse

   -ing form: avoid, consider, imagine, involve, mention, practise, suggest

2 1 refused   2 managed   3 deserved   4 pretended   5 avoid   6 considered

3 1 agreed, to come / go   2 asked, I would help   3 explained, to do / we must do   4 enquired, left / leaves   5 warned, to be   6 told, was   7 apologised, was   8 wondered, had said

Vocabulary

1 stock, catalogues   2 bargain, sale   3 guarantee, goods   4 exchange, debit

Reading and Use of English Part 4

Exam task

1 was overtaken by Frank

2 Does anyone know where my

3 Luke should do

4 would ('d) have phoned

5 doesn't / won't let me

6 had such a quiet

Unit 8

Reading and Use of English Part 6

1 **1** True **2** True **3** False – between 10 and 15 minutes
4 True **5** False – 18 days, 21 hours and 40 minutes
6 False – 9.25 hours

Exam task

1 G **2** A **3** F **4** D **5** B **6** E

Vocabulary

breathing – lungs, consciousness – brain, diet – weight,
genetics – cells, hearing – ears, sight – eyes, skeleton – bones,
smell – nose, touch – skin

Grammar

1 The book (**which / that**) **I read** yesterday was very
interesting.

2 Paul lives in the house over there **which / that** has a red front
door.

3 I didn't understand everything (**that**) the teacher said in maths
today.

4 I'd like to meet people **who / that** have the same interests as
me.

5 The star had been replaced by another actor, **who** didn't have
his talent.

6 I have been to the United States twice, **which** enabled me to
improve my English.

7 There was a very high window in the room **which / that** was
almost impossible to open.

8 I don't know the name of the boy **who is / who's** sitting in the
front row.

9 At the zoo, I took pictures of animals **which / that** are in
danger.

10 The teacher said we could leave early, **which** we all thought
was a good idea.

Reading and Use of English Part 3

1 **1** attractive **2** communicative **3** creative **4** decisive
5 decorative **6** effective **7** extensive **8** impressive
9 offensive **10** productive **11** progressive **12** protective

2 **1** artistic **2** athletic **3** atomic **4** economic **5** enthusiastic
6 historic **7** pessimistic **8** realistic

3 **1** belief **2** choice **3** death **4** gift **5** knowledge
6 marriage **7** proof **8** laughter **9** sight **10** speech
11 thought **12** success **13** freedom **14** length **15** height
16 pride **17** strength **18** width

Exam task

1 visible **2** brightness **3** dramatic **4** locations **5** impressive
6 electricity **7** inconvenient **8** harmful

Listening Part 1

a) 2, 5, 7 **b)** 1 **c)** 3, 4, 6, 8

Exam task

1 A **2** B **3** C **4** C **5** B **6** A **7** A **8** B

Recording script

*You will hear people talking in eight different situations. For
questions 1–8, choose the best answer (A, B or C). Play the
recording twice.*

1

You hear two friends talking.

Girl: So, what did you think about that new crime thriller
then?

Boy: Great. I liked the detective, he was really cool. The
things he said were really amusing, and detectives aren't
usually funny, are they?

Girl: Yeah, he made me laugh too. And I liked the
descriptions I read of him, you know, his character, the
way he dresses. I could imagine what he would look
like …

Boy: I hope they turn it into a TV series. It'd be good to have
something like that to watch every week.

Girl: Yeah, they might just turn it into a film though, <u>there's
only one book I think</u>.

Boy: Well, it'd make a great film, the plot's brilliant … so many
twists and turns …

2

You hear a boy talking about a new video game.

Boy: … yeah, I tried out the new game called *Search*
yesterday and it's brilliant. There's the usual action
stuff in it … you know, chases and swinging from
buildings and things, which lots of other games do
just as well. But there's some very clever stuff too,
like, there are all sorts of puzzles to solve before you
can move on to the next level. <u>You really have to use
your brain for those</u>. I thought they were cool and well
… a bit different really, you know, challenging. The
graphics were good too, but they always are from that
company. They're the ones that made *Mountain Run* …

3

You hear a teacher talking to his students.

Man: Hi again, everyone. I'm sure you've remembered that
we've got Joanna Sedley from the local paper coming to
talk to us tomorrow morning, about how she became a
journalist. If you think of any questions to ask while she's
speaking, she'll answer them at the end. The reason I'm
here now is that <u>I need you to set the furniture up</u>. We'll
have circles of chairs, and I'd like you to help with that
before you leave, please. Oh, and by the way, Joanna
used to be a pupil here, back in the 1990s. I think the
school might have changed a bit since then, don't you?

4

You hear a girl leaving a phone message for her mother.

Girl: Hi, Mum. It's Susie. <u>Just thought I'd let you know what
was happening</u>. I'm going to be at college for another
couple of hours. I'll be home about seven. I've missed
the bus but there's no need to come and pick me up,
because Jane's Mum's giving me a lift home. We're
still practising for the show, and then we've got to try
our costumes on, so it's all taking forever. Anyway,
the costumes look great, so that's the good news. I'm
starving though, so could you keep me some supper,
please? Great, thanks, see you later.

5

You hear a girl telling a friend about her new art teacher.

Girl 1: Have you started your art classes yet?

Girl 2: Yeah, we've had about six now with the new teacher.

Girl 1: How's that going?

Girl 2: Good actually. She's very different from Mr Jones. He always wanted us to do things his way, you know, use the same techniques, work in a particular range of colours. Mrs Boyd is very relaxed. <u>She lets us do things our way, and then comes and helps us improve</u>. It's a good way of doing things. Then she shows us what well-known artists have done after we've done our own work ... so we can compare ideas I suppose ...

Girl 1: Great!

6

You hear a career advisor talking to a group of students.

Woman: Good morning everyone. This is the stage in your education when you have choices to make about the subjects and qualifications you do. There are certain subjects you'll all study for the next two years, such as maths, science and English. I know some of you've been thinking long and hard about other subjects and qualifications, and talking things through with your parents and teachers. And of course some of you have already chosen a career, so that will influence you. However, experience shows that <u>the best plan is to take qualifications in a good number of different subjects</u>, so you keep your career options open. Here's an example ...

7

You hear two students talking at school.

Boy: Hi, Laurie. How's it going?

Girl: <u>I like a lesson like this where you have to do things</u> rather than use books! I spent hours reading this morning. We've just started a new novel in my literature course.

Boy: Yeah, I prefer being hands-on. How did your <u>experiment</u> go?

Girl: OK. Look, <u>the stuff in the tube here is the right colour.</u>

Boy: Yeah, it looks like mine anyway. What about the school play – are you helping with it again?

Girl: I'd like to. I loved helping with the scenery last term, it was kind of well, creative.

Boy: You know there's a meeting after school tomorrow? I'm going.

Girl: Right, I'll go too then.

Boy: Cool!

8

You hear a boy starting to give a talk to his class.

Boy: Well, I'm going to do my talk on lions. I hope you'll like it. African lions are such beautiful animals, and they're very much under threat, from hunting and changes to the climate. So, what I'm going to do is this: I'll begin by showing you some pictures of them, so you can understand exactly what I see in them. Then I'll tell you something about lions in general, and the lion family I watched in a safari park in Kenya. I hope you'll find it interesting. I think the way they live in big groups is fascinating, and every single lion has its own personality. That really surprised me.

Vocabulary

The ten expressions are: backup, bookmark, download, hard drive, login, password, restart, spreadsheet, update, webcam

F	H	K	P	E	Q	V	N	L	X	A	W	B	F	D
S	Y	U	G	K	U	R	T	M	Z	V	B	O	O	D
G	N	H	H	L	U	A	X	H	J	R	S	O	K	W
H	K	R	W	S	P	Z	O	I	A	E	L	K	Y	U
S	P	R	E	A	D	S	H	E	E	T	W	M	T	P
C	A	F	B	F	A	F	Y	U	D	A	F	A	E	Q
V	S	Z	C	X	T	V	A	S	F	T	G	R	S	N
J	S	I	A	C	E	Q	S	T	B	A	C	K	U	P
F	W	J	M	Y	T	O	R	B	X	X	T	I	C	R
A	O	K	M	J	S	G	R	E	S	T	A	R	T	I
E	R	H	D	L	A	L	E	M	G	B	U	O	B	S
Y	D	O	W	N	L	O	A	D	H	H	A	P	H	T
R	L	D	B	M	I	G	P	H	I	O	E	M	K	E
H	A	R	D	D	R	I	V	E	L	Z	C	D	M	A
C	N	T	P	B	K	N	G	L	N	D	V	A	A	P

Writing extra key

Unit 1

1 1 For that reason   2 For example   3 As for   4 In contrast
   5 though

2 A 2, 7, 8   B 4, 6, 10   C 1, 5   D 3, 9

3 1 due to / owing to   2 In addition / Moreover / Furthermore
   3 with the aim of / with a view to   4 in order to
   5 As a result / Therefore

4 1 owing to   2 in order to   3 with a view to   4 as a result
   5 with the aim of   6 Furthermore,   7 therefore
   8 with a view to   9 In addition   10 Due to

Unit 2

1 1 & 2 John is probably on a beach somewhere, and the boat
         is coming to rescue him. He's possibly on a desert
         island. Perhaps his boat had sunk because he'd been
         attacked by pirates or a shark. Or perhaps he'd fallen
         asleep and then fallen overboard.

2 Student's own story

3 The correct order is: 1 E   2 B   3 A   4 D   5 C

4 A had, sank, was   B had gone / went, was / had been
   taking, hit / had hit   C (had) had to, had passed, had
   changed, was coming   D realised, was, found, learned /
   learnt   E had been, had almost given up.

5 It's all right to give a story an open ending like this in the
   exam. A, B, D and E are all possible answers, i.e. you can
   think of a story that would fit. C is extremely unlikely.
   Pirates wouldn't come and rescue someone! (Or would
   they? What would be their motive?) D is less likely than the
   others as the race is likely to have been over for some time.

6 1 until   2 after   3 ago   4 during   5 since   6 before
   7 for   8 When

Unit 3

1 1 E   2 F   3 C   4 D   5 A   6 B

2 1 H   2 G   3 E   4 C   5 A   6 D   7 B   8 F

   I'd say that 'The Hound of the Baskervilles' is a book
   you really must read. The story takes place in a lonely and
   deserted place and the descriptions of it make you feel as if
   you are really there. I found the book quite frightening in
   places and as a result of that I decided never to read it late
   at night! Yet you are entertained because the writer builds
   up the atmosphere so skilfully.

   At times things happen which make you think that the
   hound, a giant dog that is supposed to haunt the area, is
   supernatural. In fact it is not, and more importantly, this
   myth of a ghostly hound is being used as a way to frighten
   and kill people so that someone can inherit a large amount
   of money.

   The famous detective Sherlock Holmes eventually finds
   the truth with the help of his good friend Dr Watson, and you
   wonder what would have happened if they had not gone to
   investigate.

   In conclusion, I would say that in my opinion, 'The
   Hound of the Baskervilles' is an outstanding book. Once you
   start reading it, you won't be able to put it down!

3 awful N   brilliant P   dreadful N   dull N
   entertaining P   fantastic P   fascinating P   horrible N
   intelligent P   stupid N   terrible N   wonderful P

4 1 brilliant   2 entertaining   3 dreadful   4 dull   5 stupid
   6 wonderful

Unit 4

1 A 2, 5   B 4, 6   C 3, 10   D 1, 8   E 7, 9

2 1 F   2 I   3 F   4 I   5 F   6 F   7 I   8 I   9 F   10 I

3 1 G being   2 D handed   3 A leaves   4 C take   5 H will
   work   6 B attend   7 F rush / rushing   8 E was

4 1 should have written   2 must have thought   3 could have
   done   4 must have been planning   5 should have worn /
   been wearing   6 must have frozen / been freezing   7 would
   / could have been   8 could / should have read

Unit 5

1 1 energetic   2 brave   3 confident   4 decisive   5 honest
   6 patient   7 responsible   8 loyal   9 caring
   10 sympathetic

2 1 O   2 E   3 O   4 E   5 E   6 O   7 O   8 E

3 1 true   2 explains   3 main   4 touching   5 turns   6 place
   7 factual   8 based   9 motivated   10 recommend

Unit 6

2 1 the one I'd most like to visit
   2 why I would choose
   3 moved here from Italy
   4 it has always sounded
   5 with a lovely climate
   6 with a long history
   7 such as those of
   8 one final argument

3 The writer talks about: the people, history, language, climate
   and food.

4 The students should underline:
   1 You are probably wondering … ; Italy is a very old country,
   isn't it?

2 My grandparents are always talking about their homeland
... and other references to grandparents, plus writer's ideas
about climate

3 ... many different civilisations such as those of the Greeks,
Etruscans and Romans.

4 I could eat my way around the country!

5 1 can't you? **2** won't you? **3** wasn't he? **4** hasn't she?
5 should you? **6** doesn't he? **7** didn't we? **8** does she?

6 1 couldn't we **2** wasn't it **3** didn't he **4** shouldn't you
5 aren't they **6** is it **7** shall we **8** aren't I **9** is he
10 will you / won't you

Unit 7

1 1 the kind that **2** such as **3** until recently **4** even if
5 because **6** instead **7** As a result **8** Then

2 1 fashion and shopping

2 paragraphs: **a** – second paragraph **b** – first paragraph
c – third paragraph

3 Beginning: 3, 5, 6 End: 1, 2, 4

4 Students' own answers

5 1 D **2** E **3** F **4** C **5** A **6** B

6 Model answer

Dear Paul

You asked me to write about clothes in my country and to
tell you whether both boys and girls are interested in them.
I have to say that I think they are. That's because I live in
France, where the way you look is important to everyone.
From a young age we all want to choose the right clothes
and wear fashionable colours.

Jeans are popular for both boys and girls in my country, but
they have to fit well and be the right colour! You need to
be comfortable, but at the same time, you must look good.
When we relax at the weekend we simply wear jeans and
T-shirts, and a hoodie or jumper when we are cold. Girls
and boys wear similar things around the house.

However, when we dress up for a special occasion, we look
very different. The girls wear a brightly-coloured dress,
and some sandals or shoes. The boys wear a colourful shirt,
and as they get older, a jacket. Everyone makes an effort,
because that is part of our culture. As a result, we dress
well.

I hope I've given you the information you need.

Best wishes

Toni

Unit 8

1 Suggested answers

1 Unhealthy foods: biscuits, cakes, chips, ice cream

2 These foods contain protein: fish, eggs, meat and nuts

2 1 A **2** F **3** A **4** F **5** F **6** A

3 1 O **2** P **3** P **4** O **5** O **6** P **7** O

4 1 but **2** Moreover / In fact **3** because **4** in fact /
moreover **5** if **6** However **7** so **8** in order to

5 Model answer

It is my personal belief that meat isn't good for your health
if you eat large quantities. In addition, I don't think it is
right that we spend millions of pounds feeding animals
when people in some parts of the world have nothing to eat.
I think it is unlikely that everyone will become vegetarian,
but eating less meat less often would be a good start.

Progress test 1 Units 1–2

1 Use a form of the word in capitals to complete each sentence.

1 What are you planning for my birthday? You're being very .... about it.
MYSTERY

2 The night sky is .... clear in large cities.
RARE

3 Don't ask Fred to help you as he's not very

....
RELY

4 I was .... when I found out what had happened.
FURY

5 The hotel room was only .... because we had air-conditioning.
BEAR

6 Alison does her piano practice quite .... every day after school.
HAPPY

7 I don't think your argument is very ....
LOGIC

8 The decision to build a new housing estate has been rather ....
CONTROVERSY

9 You've made .... progress since you joined the class.
REMARK

10 .... we'll be able to go to the beach tomorrow.
HOPEFUL

2 Choose the best answer (a, b or c) to complete each sentence.

1 We live in a(n) .... eighteenth-century town. There are some fascinating old things to see.
a historic
b antique
c ancient

2 We often go hiking .... the mountains.
a on
b at
c in

3 Dan goes swimming .... twice a week.
a at first
b at least
c at last

4 I .... you to do your best.
a demand
b expect
c believe

5 Alice likes living in the middle of .... because it's so quiet.
a everywhere
b somewhere
c nowhere

6 Tom is so .... He really thinks he's better than everyone else.
a arrogant
b annoyed
c doubtful

7 I have no idea at .... why you want to live in the city centre!
a once
b last
c all

8 My parents' house is not far .... the coast.
a of
b from
c away

9 We stayed in a .... fishing village last summer. It was so quiet.
a crowded
b rural
c sleepy

10 The streets in the centre of Washington are really .... , unlike Cambridge where they are very narrow.
a wide
b deep
c long

3 Complete each sentence with a suitable form of the words in the box.

big	bad	tall	expensive	happy	good
exciting	far				

1 My brother is .... me. He's 1m 80 and I'm only 1m 60.

2 I think Tokyo must be .... city in the world. I spent a fortune when I went there last year.

3 What's .... holiday you've ever had? Mine was in Canada. It was absolutely fantastic.

4 Sally looks .... she used to because she's got a new job. She's certainly smiling more!

5 Yuk! That's one of .... meals I've ever eaten. It was absolutely disgusting.

6 Activity holidays are certainly .... beach holidays in my opinion.

7 Maria doesn't like travelling. In fact, she's never been .... the capital.

8 Our new house is .... our last one. It only had two bedrooms whereas our new one has four.

4 Choose the best answer.

1 *I'll call / I call* you when I've heard from Mark.

2 We will be very busy when our cousins *will come / come* next week.

3 Look at the sky. *It's going to / It'll* rain any minute now.

4 I think *I'll / I'm going to* have fish for lunch today.

5 What time *will / does* your flight leave tomorrow?

6 We *celebrate / are celebrating* Hannah's birthday this weekend.

7 The newspaper says the film *doesn't / won't* start until 6.00 so we've got plenty of time.

8 Please let me know as soon as you*'ll decide / decide* what you want to do.

9 *I'm going to / I'll* pick you up at the airport if you give me your flight details.

10 *Will you be spending / Do you spend* any time with your relatives this summer?

5 Complete the email with the correct form of the verbs in brackets.

Hi Jake!

How are you? I'm sorry I (**1**) .... (**write**) for ages but we only (**2**) .... (**get**) back from our holiday on Sunday and since then I (**3**) .... (**try**) to finish off some school work. We (**4**) .... (**have**) a fantastic time! We (**5**) .... (**fly**) to Seattle and then we (**6**) .... (**take**) a ferry to Vancouver Island. After we (**7**) .... (**be**) there for a week, we (**8**) .... (**meet**) up with my aunt and uncle. They (**9**) .... (**rent**) a house on the island for a few years because they love the climate, though one day there (**10**) .... (**be**) a huge storm while we (**11**) .... (**enjoy**) a picnic on the beach. Scary!

I really (**12**) .... (**want**) to come back home and hope I can go and visit them again next year.

Write soon,

Kevin

Progress test 2 Units 3-4

1 Choose the best answer (a, b or c) to complete each sentence.

1 A .... performs the action scenes in a film.
  a director
  b cameraman
  c stuntman

2 What does a .... technician do?
  a sound
  b make-up
  c costume

3 *Mamma Mia* was filmed on .... on one of the beautiful Greek islands.
  a location
  b set
  c scenery

4 I enjoy watching .... about natural history.
  a action films
  b westerns
  c documentaries

5 I like to have a good laugh at the cinema so .... are my favourite.
  a comedies
  b horror films
  c science-fiction films

6 The .... used to create the magic tricks in the *Harry Potter* films are incredibly realistic.
  a actors
  b special effects
  c stunts

7 I think heavy metal music only appeals to a certain age ....
  a gang
  b band
  c group

8 I found the .... of that film we watched yesterday really difficult to follow.
  a casting
  b plot
  c acting

2 Choose the best answer.

1 *Although / In spite* I enjoy going to the cinema, I prefer watching DVDs at home.

2 Brad Pitt is a great actor. *While / However*, his last film was a little disappointing.

3 Chris and Steve play the guitar *while / despite* their brother Dan plays the drums.

4 *In spite of / Even though* having a lot of experience, John hasn't been able to get a job.

5 *Even though / Despite* her father was a great actor, Julia didn't enjoy watching his films.

6 *However / Despite* the bad reviews, the film was still very successful.

7 Kiera Knightley has appeared in a lot of films. Her latest one, *however / although*, was not particularly good.

8 *In spite / Despite* the fact that I don't like thrillers, I went to see one with my best friend.

3 Rewrite the sentences in the passive.

1 They're showing my favourite film on TV this evening.
....

2 George Lucas directed most of the *Star Wars* films.
....

3 They will release Jessie J's new album soon.
....

4 You can buy the latest films quite cheaply on the Internet.
....

5 How much money did they spend on the music extravaganza?
....

6 They make hundreds of Bollywood films every year.
....

7 That local group have recorded several albums.
....

8 The Arctic Monkeys are going to open the musical festival.
....

4 Complete each sentence with one of the words in the box.

race   snowboarding   track   badminton
umpire   net   goalkeeper   opponent
gymnastics   ice skating

1 The .... saved a penalty and Barcelona went on to win the match.

2 The spectators at the tennis match were quite noisy so the .... found it difficult to keep order.

3 It's always satisfying when you can beat your ....

4 Max goes .... in the Alps as soon as there's enough snow.

5 I gave up .... after I hurt my back.

6 The local athletics .... is very popular.

7 The four of us used to play .... regularly at the leisure centre.

8 Jamie served a double fault and the ball went into the ....

9 There's a rink near us so I often go .... at the weekend.

10 Matt came last in the 200m .... but he didn't mind.

5 Choose the best answer.

1 It's important to have a *balanced / tough* diet if you want to be healthy.

2 Yum!! That pizza was really *salty / tasty*. How did you make it so delicious?

3 I only buy *rich / seasonal* vegetables because I know they're grown locally.

4 Most fast foods are quite *fatty / fried* so they're not very good for you.

5 That chocolate cake was very *ripe / rich*. How could you eat two pieces?!

6 I forgot to put the strawberries in the fridge so now most of them are *tough / rotten*.

6 Rewrite the sentences using *You* + the word in brackets.

1 Is it necessary to wear a school uniform? (have)
....

2 It's a good idea to study every day. (should)
....

3 It isn't possible to play football after school. (can't)
....

4 It is possible that you saw Helen yesterday. (could)
....

5 It is forbidden to take reference books from the library. (mustn't)
....

6 It isn't necessary to bring your sports kit to school today. (have)
....

7 It wasn't good that you shouted at the referee. (shouldn't)
....

8 It's possible that you won't get a ticket as the band are very popular. (might)
....

9 You were able to swim when you were five, weren't you? (could)
....

10 It is necessary to practise every day. (must)
....

Progress test 3 Units 5–6

1 Complete each sentence with one of the words in the box.

> uniform   timetable   library   history
> geography   primary   rules   science

1 In England pupils usually go to .... school when they are five or six.

2 We have to wear a .... at our school.

3 Ben really enjoys .... because he's interested in the past.

4 You can take up to six books out of the .... at any one time.

5 According to my .... , our next lesson is IT.

6 We're learning about South America in our .... lessons.

7 Why do we have to study .... ? I'm not interested in chemistry and physics.

8 You have to obey the .... if you want to stay out of trouble.

2 Rewrite the sentences using the word in brackets.

1 Joe won't go to university if he doesn't pass all his exams. (unless)

....

2 I studied French because I wanted to spend some time in France. (wouldn't)

....

3 Children pay more attention because they eat healthily. (If)

....

4 I don't enjoy school so I don't do well. (If)

....

5 I want the rain to stop. (wish)

....

6 I regret failing my maths exam. (wish)

....

7 We'll take our cameras because we might see some famous people. (case)

....

8 I'll provide the food for the picnic if you make some lemonade. (long)

....

9 I'm sorry that I don't have my own laptop. (only)

....

10 I play tennis well because I practise every day. (didn't)

....

3 Choose the best answer (**a, b** or **c**) to complete each sentence.

1 Monkeys normally live in the .... where they can find plenty of food and shelter.
   a grassland
   b jungle
   c desert

2 I try to recycle as much of my .... as possible.
   a rubbish
   b package
   c litter

3 David .... very green so he saves envelopes and string and reuses them.
   a has
   b is
   c lives

4 When was the last time the .... erupted?
   a volcano
   b hurricane
   c pollution

5 The snow and ice in Antarctica are .... due to changes in global temperature.
   a flooding
   b warming
   c melting

6 People living close to airports often have to .... the noise of aircraft taking off at night.
   a put up with
   b look up to
   c come up with

7 Due to the lack of ...., the farmers have lost a lot of their crops.
   a rainfall
   b storms
   c drought

8 Some houses are more .... to the installation of solar panels than others.
   a fitted
   b matched
   c suited

9 Thanks to industrial ...., no fish can survive in the local river.
   a environment
   b pollution
   c climate

10 The rivers are slowly drying .... in the heat.
   a up
   b off
   c out

4 Choose the best answer.

1 Could you give me a *slice* / *piece* of paper, please?

2 Would you like *some* / *a* bread with your soup?

3 I don't have *much* / *many* free time at the moment.

4 There are only a *few* / *little* cars in our village.

5 We didn't have a *little* / *much* homework this week.

6 I'm going to the funfair because I want *some* / *an* excitement.

7 *Much* / *Many* of the news is really depressing.

8 Can I give you *some* / *an* advice?

9 We don't usually get *many* / *much* snow in London.

10 How *many* / *much* exercise do you do every day?

5 Complete the text with one word in each gap.

Did you have (1)............................ favourite subject at school? I did and mine (2)............................ French. Our teacher, Mrs Laurent, was (3)............................ an inspirational woman that I decided to study French at university. However, my exam results weren't quite good (4)............................, so I had to do (5)............................ else. I decided to do some travelling and I spent several months in (6)............................ Amazon where I helped with (7)............................ project studying the effects of deforestation upon (8)............................ local environment. Now I'm working with (9)............................ agency in London and I spend most of my time organising campaigns. Unfortunately, I'm (10)............................ busy to travel at the moment but I'm hoping to go back to Brazil soon. It's (11)............................ interesting that I would like to spend as (12)............................ time as possible there!

Progress test 4 Units 7–8

1 Complete the sentences with the correct form of the verbs in brackets.

1 After playing football for her school team for two years, Jane went on .... (become) captain.

2 Please let me .... (help) you with your homework.

3 We look forward to .... (see) you at the party on Saturday.

4 Sally's interested in .... (study) fashion design.

5 I'd prefer .... (go) home now if you don't mind.

6 Mum persuaded me .... (not give up) my course.

7 I don't remember .... (buy) that T-shirt. Are you sure it's not yours?

8 Paul suggested .... (join) the local gym.

9 Don't forget .... (give) me your new mobile number.

10 I enjoy .... (not have) to do any homework during the school holidays.

2 Choose the correct alternative.

1 Stephen only wears *smart* / *everyday* clothes when he goes to visit his grandmother.

2 I don't have much money so I often buy *designer* / *second-hand* clothes.

3 I'm so embarrassed when I go into town with Harry. He wears such *outrageous* / *individual* clothes.

4 Lisa thinks she's really cool but actually her clothes are extremely *unfashionable* / *vintage*.

5 I tend to wear *casual* / *colourful* clothes when the weather's dull and grey because it makes me feel brighter.

6 Diana always looks very *well-designed* / *elegant* even when she isn't doing anything special.

3 Complete each sentence with one of the words in the box.

amused   concerned   curious   furious   guilty   upset

1 I was absolutely .... when I found out what Emma had done.

2 Sally was understandably .... that John forgot her birthday. She looked very sad.

3 Dan's a .... little boy, always asking questions.

4 You must have done something wrong. You're looking really ....

5 I'm quite .... about Alex because he looks exhausted most of the time.

6 Luckily, Lucy was .... when she realised we were both wearing the same dress to Paul's wedding.

4 Rewrite the sentences with the prompts.

1 'Clare, don't forget to call David.'
Sally reminded ....

2 'Why did Stephen leave so suddenly?'
Mary asked ....

3 'Are the boys going to play tennis later?'
Val asked ....

4 'I've never been to Canada.'
Dan told ....

5 'You should study harder, Laura.'
Harry advised ....

6 'Why don't you try for the school team, Rob?'
Simon encouraged ....

7 'We can meet you at 6.00.'
Frieda said ....

8 'Mark was playing the piano when I called round.'
Fred told me ....

5 Choose the best answer (a, b or c) to complete each sentence.

1 We're studying the human body in ....
   a physics
   b biology
   c ecology

2 If we used public transport more often, there wouldn't be so much ....
   a pollution
   b ecosystem
   c conservation

3 How many trillions of .... are there in the human brain?
   a acids
   b genetics
   c cells

4 Hundreds of .... are added to the endangered list every year.
   a genetics
   b ecosystems
   c species

5 I'm sure we'll all have .... to help us tidy our houses soon.
   a robots
   b plastics
   c atoms

6 We do algebra and geometry in ....
   a chemistry
   b maths
   c biology

7 The speed of .... is slower than the speed of light.
   a sound
   b heat
   c electricity

8 .... are used to reflect light.
   a Cells
   b Mirrors
   c Gases

9 You need a .... to access the Internet.
   a spreadsheet
   b webcam
   c browser

10 Click on the yellow .... to open up the program.
   a email
   b icon
   c webcam

6 Use a form of the word in capitals to complete each sentence.

1 Dan's really .... and always has to win.
   COMPETE

2 You will be punished for your ....
   HONEST

3 What's the .... of that suitcase?
   WEIGH

4 I've never understood the .... of hip-hop.
   POPULAR

5 In the UK, it's .... to drive before the age of 17.
   LEGAL

6 There have been some .... in the plans for the new school.
   DEVELOP

7 I'm afraid there's been a .... I do apologise.
   UNDERSTAND

8 I don't want the .... of making the final decision.
   RESPONSIBLE

9 You could .... have hurt yourself.
   EASY

10 Anna got no .... at all from learning a long list of dates by heart for her history test.
   SATISFY

Progress tests key

Progress test 1

1 1 mysterious 2 rarely 3 reliable 4 furious 5 bearable 6 happily 7 logical 8 controversial 9 remarkable 10 Hopefully

2 1 a 2 c 3 b 4 b 5 c 6 a 7 c 8 b 9 c 10 a

3 1 bigger / taller than 2 the most expensive 3 the best / most exciting 4 happier than 5 the worst 6 more exciting / better than 7 further than 8 bigger than

4 1 I'll call 2 come 3 It's going to 4 I'll 5 does 6 are celebrating 7 doesn't 8 decide 9 I'll 10 Will you be spending

5 1 haven't written 2 got 3 've (have) been trying 4 had 5 flew 6 took 7 had been 8 met 9 've (have) been renting 10 was 11 were enjoying 12 didn't want

Progress test 2

1 1 c 2 a 3 a 4 c 5 a 6 b 7 c 8 b

2 1 Although 2 However 3 while 4 In spite of 5 Even though 6 Despite 7 however 8 Despite

3 1 My favourite film is being shown on TV this evening.
2 Most of the *Star Wars* films were directed by George Lucas.
3 Jessie J's new album will be released soon.
4 The latest films can be bought quite cheaply on the Internet.
5 How much money was spent on the musical extravaganza?
6 Hundreds of Bollywood films are made every year.
7 Several albums have been recorded by that local group.
8 The music festival is going to be opened by the Arctic Monkeys.

4 1 goalkeeper 2 umpire 3 opponent 4 snowboarding 5 gymnastics 6 track 7 badminton 8 net 9 ice skating 10 race

5 1 balanced 2 tasty 3 seasonal 4 fatty 5 rich 6 rotten

6 1 Do you have to wear a school uniform?
2 You should study every day.
3 You can't play football after school.
4 You could have seen Helen yesterday.
5 You mustn't take reference books from the library.
6 You don't have to bring your sports kit to school today.
7 You shouldn't have shouted at the referee.
8 You might not get a ticket as the band are very popular.
9 You could swim when you were five, couldn't you?
10 You must practise every day.

Progress test 3

1 1 primary 2 uniform 3 history 4 library 5 timetable 6 geography 7 science 8 rules

2 1 Joe won't go to university unless he passes all his exams.
2 I wouldn't have studied French if I hadn't wanted to spend some time in France.
3 If children eat healthily, they pay more attention.
4 If I enjoyed school, I would do well. OR If I enjoy school, I will do well.
5 I wish the rain would stop. OR I wish it would stop raining.
6 I wish I hadn't failed / had passed my maths exam.
7 We'll take our cameras in case we see some famous people.
8 I'll provide the food for the picnic as long as you make some lemonade.
9 If only I had my own laptop.
10 I wouldn't play tennis well if I didn't practise every day.

3 1 b 2 a 3 b 4 a 5 c 6 a 7 a 8 c 9 b 10 a

4 1 piece 2 some 3 much 4 few 5 much 6 some 7 Much 8 some 9 much 10 much

5 1 a 2 was 3 such 4 enough 5 something 6 the 7 a 8 the 9 an 10 too 11 so 12 much

Progress test 4

1 **1** to become **2** help **3** seeing **4** studying **5** to go
6 not to give up **7** buying **8** joining **9** to give
10 not having

2 **1** smart **2** second-hand **3** outrageous
4 unfashionable **5** colourful **6** elegant

3 **1** furious **2** upset **3** curious **4** guilty **5** concerned
6 amused

4 **1** Sally reminded Clare to call David.

2 Mary asked why Stephen had left so suddenly.

3 Val asked whether / if the boys were going to play tennis
later.

4 Dan told me he'd never been to Canada.

5 Harry advised Laura to study harder.

6 Simon encouraged Rob to try for the school team.

7 Frieda said they could meet me / us at 6.00.

8 Fred told me (that) Mark had been playing the piano when
he'd called round.

5 **1** b **2** a **3** c **4** c **5** a **6** b **7** a **8** b **9** c **10** b

6 **1** competitive **2** dishonesty **3** weight **4** popularity
5 illegal **6** developments **7** misunderstanding
8 responsibility **9** easily **10** satisfaction

Photocopiable resources

Unit 1, Speaking, Part 1, Exercise 2

Examiner: Hello, George. I'm going to ask you some questions about yourself. Do you do any activities after school?

George: Yes, I do. I'm learning to dive so I have a lesson every Wednesday after school in the pool. That's my favourite time in the whole week.

Examiner: When do you do your homework?

George: When I get home from school, I watch TV. I like to relax for an hour so I prefer to do my homework after dinner.

Examiner: Francesca, what do you usually do at the weekend?

Francesca: I usually meet my friends in the city centre on Saturdays and we spend all afternoon shopping and chatting. On Sunday mornings, I go to see my grandmother.

Examiner: What are you going to do next weekend?

Francesca: On Saturday I'm going to get the bus to town with my friends as usual and we'll probably go to the cinema. But on Sunday I'll be practising my guitar most of the day as I'm playing in a concert next Tuesday. I know I need to practise a lot before that!

Unit 1, Speaking, Part 2, Exercise 8

Francesca: In both of the photographs the people are exercising but I think the people in the first photograph are much happier than the people in the second one. They're riding their bikes in the countryside whereas the people in the second photo are indoors on the running machines in the gym, which isn't as enjoyable as being in the fresh air. Also, in the gym they are doing things separately instead of having fun together. On the other hand, they are probably getting more exercise as they are being more energetic than the people in the first photograph. In the first photograph there is a group of friends or maybe cousins even and they're excited about going somewhere together. They're probably chatting as well. They'll spend less money than going to the gym as cycling is free.

Unit 2, Listening, Part 1, Exercise 4

Girl: Well, it's my hometown and I love it! People eat out quite a lot here and you'll find everything from Brazilian food to Spanish tapas. But if I go out with my family, we usually eat Italian: pasta and pizza. What I find absolute magic about the city though is the street celebrations – they take place all year. In winter, when the snow falls and the days get shorter, we have the Lights Festival in the main square, which is really fantastic. And then of course there's the underground city which is basically a huge shopping mall. I often go there with my sister – she just adores it, but I find it a bit too big!

Unit 4, Listening, Part 2, Exam task

I'm training very hard at the moment because I'm hoping to be picked for the Olympic ice-skating team. I should have been in the team four years ago – well, that's what my coach said. But I was left out, so I'm determined to be selected this time. I competed in a national championship last week and so did my brother – he skates too. Jack Graham was defending the title – you might have seen him on TV afterwards – and he must have been practising all the time as he was even better than last year and finished first. But I was second, just behind him, and my brother came third so we were both pleased. Either of us could have won but you just never know who's going to do best on the day.

To be good enough to win competitions, I need to be really fit. Obviously I practise every day and I spend a lot of my time on the ice doing spins and jumps to get them exactly right. But I skate really badly if I ever forget to stretch. That's really crucial and something all skaters have to do, so I spend about thirty or forty minutes doing that every day before and after I go on the ice. It keeps me flexible as well as free from injury.

I enjoy competitions but I do get nervous, so I never think about the skaters I'm competing against. I just focus on the audience and hope they're enjoying it – then I skate well. If I start thinking about the judges, then I make mistakes.

And something new for me, I'm going to be a judge myself soon. I always loved the TV show *Ice Champions* when I was a child and now I'm going to be one of the judges of *Stars on Ice*, which is for teenagers. I'd say to any contestant wanting to do well, you should build up your confidence so that you put on a really smooth and entertaining show. Each skater has a partner. They can't choose who they skate with and they have to follow a certain routine, but they can decide which music they want to skate to.

I'm hoping one day to have more time for hobbies. I go swimming whenever I can – that was my first love before skating and it helps me with my moves on the ice. I'd love to go horse riding or play tennis, but although they would be good for building up muscles and fitness, I can't fit everything in! And now I need to go and do some training …

Unit 5, Listening, Part 2, Exercise 9

Well, I'm going to talk about my visit to the Aeroseum in Gothenburg in Sweden. I went there with my technology class. It was really interesting and we all enjoyed it. We arrived about half past nine in the morning and we were met by our guide, who fortunately spoke very good English!

The museum is located in some underground shelters not far from a former airport, which was used by the military. Building the shelters was a huge project. Work started in the 1940s and then continued in the 1950s. The guide told us that they had to carve out and move tons of rock, which is much harder than digging out earth. And we found out later that no-one knew anything about the existence of the shelters till just over twenty years ago, when work on creating the museum began. That was because they didn't appear on maps and were kept secret, even from people who lived locally.

And when you enter the museum, you realise how much thought went into the design. First you have to press a button outside the main doors. As each person does this the number on the counter screen changes, so you can see exactly how many people are inside at any one time – that's a safety thing. Then there is a loud 'beep' and the doors slide open. They weigh about 180 tons and are about a metre thick, so the building would have been well defended against attack!

I was expecting to see some really old planes, so I was amazed that the first thing you see when you go in are some jets, which look as if they could have been built quite recently. I got a very clear impression of what the shelter was like when it was in active use in the 1950s. And the great thing about this museum is that nothing is off limits; you can climb into any of the exhibits. I really enjoyed getting into one of the cockpits. I was expecting the controls to be complex, but the size of it astonished me. It was so small. It must have been really hard for the pilot to cope with.

After that, our guide told us about the photo gallery, which has pictures of the site construction, and photos of the people who lived and worked in the building over the decades. I didn't find that so interesting, but later on we met a man who volunteers in the gallery now and was happy to describe his experiences of flying planes from the airport and servicing them underground. That was fascinating.

Another thing I really liked was watching people hard at work restoring some of the old planes. The amazing thing was that some of them were working on a wing, and the frame was built of wood, just like the models I've been making. Once that had been made, the wing was covered with fabric, using lots of layers to give it strength. I have to say it didn't look very strong to me, and it was very delicate work!

We stopped for refreshments and then spent more time looking at other aircraft displays before making our way through some of the service tunnels, which were used to bring in supplies, and then going to the control room, where we learned all about 'holding patterns' – the way aircraft are held above the airport, circling round until they can land. We then moved into the radio room, where another volunteer told us about his work and our visit came to a close.

I had a great time. We were there for about three hours and I have to say I could happily have stayed for much longer. I learned a lot and it was really hands on – living history; it meant something to me.

Now, I've got some photos to show you, so if you just hang on …

Unit 6, Listening, Part 4

Speaker 1

Yeah, well several of the volcanoes in my country have erupted in recent years, and thrown huge clouds of dust into the sky. This ash is dangerous for aircraft, so there have been times when airports all over Europe have had to close down. It's very dark everywhere when a volcano has just erupted. Normally, though, the weather in my country is mild all year because we're an island. Our summers don't get very hot, and our winters are rarely very cold. But because we're located between the cold air and sea of the Arctic and the warmer air and sea of the more temperate countries, we sometimes get several seasons in a day: sunshine and mild temperatures; windy, cool temperatures and rain; snow and temperatures below zero! Weird eh?!

Speaker 2

The cities in my country are getting hotter, and we get a lot of industrial pollution now. In addition, the ocean is warming, and sea levels are rising. We've always had quite a lot of flooding, during the rainy season, and that's getting worse, much more extreme. The whole continent is experiencing climate change.

I live in a very large country, so the climate varies according to where you are. For example, in the far north, there's a semi-desert with mineral deposits and fantastic game reserves with giraffes and things. That contrasts with the land along the coast which is humid and tropical, and where there's a mixture of rainforest and farmland. And finally, the areas inland are much cooler and wetter than the coast because there is regular rainfall.

Speaker 3

People often associate my country with cold weather and snow, but in fact the climate is very diverse. There are four very distinct seasons. In summer, temperatures can rise to 35°Celsius and higher, and scientists are saying that this extreme heat will increase with global warming. In winter, when most parts of the country have snow, temperatures fall as low as –25°Celsius but we manage to stay warm because we have heated houses, cars and public transportation systems. Some cities have even installed walkways to and from buildings in schools, although mine hasn't got one yet!

Spring is generally pleasant and very mild. The fall is often cool, but really bright, with rich orange and red leaves on trees. That's certainly my favourite time of year. OK, so …

Unit 6, Listening, Part 4, Exercise 9

Teacher: Tim, why did you choose to do your project on 'how to lead a greener life'?

Tim: Well, we'd done a lot about global warming and climate change in our science lessons. It was all a bit complicated really, but I knew something about the big issues. I found it all rather negative and depressing. So, I decided to think small, and see what I could do in my own life, rather than just act completely helpless. And I knew the rest of my family would be interested.

Teacher: Did you find it easy to get information?

Tim: Yeah, I discovered there were lots of people of my age blogging about being green. There was stuff about transport, and ways of getting to school each day. I'd always gone by car – Mum used to drop me off and then drive across town to work. Catching a bus would be better, from the environmental point of view, but we're not on a bus route, so I've gone for riding my bike to school now. Some of my friends live close to the school, so they can walk, but that's not possible for me.

Teacher: OK, and what about being green once you're actually at school?

Tim: Well, I looked up how schools could make better use of resources like paper. I realised that although all school paper was recycled, we used huge quantities, and I thought we should cut down. And then it came to me – it's obvious really – that we should be sending in most of our work electronically, you know, by email attachment. I'm going to recommend it to our school council – the people from each class who give the head teacher suggestions from pupils. I read about something called GOOS paper too, that's paper that's still 'good on one side', and actually most of my friends do that already – use both sides I mean.

Teacher: And what about the school cafeteria?

Tim: We could make that environmentally friendly as well. One school I've read about has 'meatless Mondays'. Apparently, if we eat less meat, we use far less of the world's resources, and animals like cows and sheep pollute the atmosphere with methane gas! It's good to use local produce too, so we don't have to transport it far. That's something our school already does. But we still have machines with bottled milk, water and juice for sale, and I think we should just have jugs of water on the tables instead.

Teacher: Did you think about life at home too?

Tim: Yeah, I think families are high energy consumers, especially now many homes are built with air conditioning. People of my age use huge amounts of power by leaving computer screens and game boxes running 24/7 – they're never turned off! Now that's something we can all do something about! Fortunately, there are improvements like energy-efficient light bulbs though, which most people now have.

Teacher: And what about water? That's a precious resource in every country in the world!

Tim: Absolutely, so we should ask ourselves whether we really need a long hot bath when we get in from playing football! Wouldn't taking a quick shower do? And hands up anyone who leaves the tap on when they brush their teeth. Do you need to do that? Of course you don't. And if you're putting your sports clothes in the washing machine, use a cold setting if you can. Your parents will be happy because you'll use less electricity!

Teacher: Did you think about shopping?

Tim: Yeah, families can do a lot to help the environment and reduce waste when they go to a food store. You don't need a new plastic bag every time you shop. You should take your own bags with you, and buy drinks in a glass bottle if you can, because glass is always recycled. It's better to cut down on food which is packaged, and if you do continue to purchase ready prepared food rather than cooking with fresh ingredients, take the cardboard packets to the recycling bank, don't just chuck them in the dustbin!

Teacher: Thanks Tim.

Unit 7, Listening, Part 3, Exam task

Speaker 1

There isn't much to do round here at weekends, so I usually go to the shopping centre with my friends. We go in loads of shops and try stuff on, it's all too expensive for us but it's something to do. Most of it looks really bad on me as I'm really tall and thin but I've got used to what kind of clothes look good on me – things like long jumpers and skinny jeans. So when I've got some money, I know exactly what to look for. I like to have my friends with me though for a second opinion.

Speaker 2

Most of my friends want to get all the latest stuff but I never really know what to buy. So when I go to get something new, I try to get what my mates are wearing. Mostly we wear jeans and hoodies and, if we can afford them, designer T-shirts. They never really go out of fashion. I like going round the shops and looking at what's there but I'm not good at deciding and I'm not very adventurous with colours and styles. When I've got a lot of money, then I might decide to keep up with the latest fashions.

Speaker 3

My mum and my sister and I often go shopping together. We have a good time, especially if my mum is feeling generous, but she obviously likes different things from me. She thinks I should wear bright cheerful things, whereas I like to wear grey or black. She also thinks that being well-dressed is really important, so I should buy things that look smart and will last but I prefer to buy cheap clothes I can replace. I love going shopping with my best friend too. We've got completely different tastes but we like getting each other's opinions all the same.

Speaker 4

It annoys me that all the shops have the same things in them, then the fashion suddenly changes and one day everybody's wearing long shorts and then the next day the latest thing is tight black jeans. Some styles really suit some people but not others, so it doesn't really work. I usually go shopping on my own because I find most of the chain stores a bit boring and I'm looking for stuff that will make me look different from my friends. I do find it eventually – sometimes it's just an unusual colour but often I invent my own fashion. Some of it might look a bit strange but I don't mind.

Speaker 5

I've been interested in clothes since I was little, when I used to argue with my mum about what I would wear – I used to refuse to wear colours that didn't match and I'm still the same. I take ages to get ready in the morning because I want to look stylish and elegant. It's not because I want people to notice me but because I feel better about myself when I've taken a bit of time. My friends like to get dressed up in their best clothes when they go out but the rest of the time they just wear jeans and a T-shirt. That's not for me.

 Compact First for Schools by Barbara Thomas and Laura Matthews ©Cambridge University Press 2014 **Photocopiable**

Unit 8, Listening, Part 1, Exam task

Question One. You hear a brother and sister talking.

Boy: Hey sis, I've lost everything I wrote yesterday and I've no idea why. Fortunately I backed it up on my memory stick, so I won't have to start again. Have you had any trouble with the laptop today?

Girl: Well, I know it's getting old, but it hasn't crashed on me or anything. I've been using it this morning and it seems OK. Hang on, is your project called 'Magnetism'?

Boy: Yeah …

Girl: Well, it's here, look, in my documents. You must have forgotten to switch user …

Boy: OK.

Girl: The Internet's slow though – I lost the connection once. I don't think broadband is very fast here in the village …

Question Two. You hear a sports programme on the radio.

Presenter: … and with another of the season's big races coming up tomorrow, conditions could be interesting … temperatures are set to fall rapidly overnight, with some mist forming. That may not clear completely by the time the race starts and that will mean some frost, so the track could be slippery. There were a few incidents during the last race today, with cars skidding and bumping into each other, so let's hope we don't get a repeat. Things will improve the day after, when sunny intervals and showers are predicted, so it will mean muddy conditions on the rugby field again at the weekend …

Question Three. You hear a teacher talking to his class.

Teacher: Well, I'm glad you've sorted out that little problem of leaving litter on the sports field, and just in time because we're holding a major hockey competition here on Saturday for all the schools in the area. We'd appreciate some help with that. We need about 20 volunteers, some in the car park to show where parents can drop players off, some indoors making sure everyone knows where the changing rooms are, and a few more to assist with refreshments half-way through the competition. I'll pass a list round. Put a tick against your name if you're willing to help …

Question Four. You hear a boy and girl talking about school.

Boy: You know I've always hated maths, Lucy, but I've done much better since we've had that new teacher. He makes it all seem logical …

Girl: Mmm, for me maths is relaxing – it's all there on the page. I don't enjoy the classes with the new teacher though. Although he is really good at explaining, he goes too far and makes it all a bit too simple. I'm not being pushed hard at all, you know, asked to do really difficult things in algebra and geometry and so on.

Boy: Well, yeah. If the class is right for me, it's not going to be right for you, is it?

Girl: I don't know about that …

Question Five. You hear a boy talking to his sister about a shopping trip.

Girl: How was the shopping trip, then?

Boy: The new computer store is great. You can't get near any of the play stations and stuff because there are so many people, but they sell some great games.

Girl: Where else did you go?

Boy: That fast food place. I lost Joe and Mike on the way there. I thought they were just playing a trick on me when they didn't reply to my texts. So I hid behind one of the little trees outside the fast food place and gave them a real shock when they walked past! I wish I hadn't done it now; they were upset because they couldn't find me.

Girl: Oh, are you still speaking?

Boy: Just about …

Question Six. You hear a girl talking to her class about her visit to an aquarium.

Girl: Well, yeah, I thought this visit was cool. I've done so many school trips to museums and there's only so many glass cases you can look at, even if you're interested in history! The exhibits here were alive. You walked through the glass tunnels in the aquarium and you could see the fish swimming just above your head. And then there was a place where you could actually touch some weird flat fish called rays, which really made the visit for me. Everyone should have a go at that if they can. There was a café which had an exhibition of lovely paintings and photos, too. They looked like the real thing I'd just seen.

Question Seven. You hear a boy talking about a cookery competition he entered.

Boy: … my catering teacher encouraged me to enter a baking competition, and I decided to make a cheesecake. You need lots of ingredients: biscuits and butter for the base, soft cheese, eggs, vanilla, sugar and cream for the filling and fresh raspberries and lemon for the sauce. I knew it was important not to forget anything. I could have played safe and made something very straightforward, but I wanted to make something that would impress. I was nervous – there were lots of competitors – and I forgot to put the cream into the filling. The cheesecake was great though – very firm. And the judges loved it – I came second. Result!

Question Eight. You hear a father and daughter talking about a holiday.

Girl: The holiday centre in Holland sounds great, Dad, but why are we hiring bikes?

Father: Well, the idea is that once you've arrived and put your luggage into the cabins, you park your vehicle and leave it. I think it's a good system but I'm wondering about getting the train there once we've taken the ferry to Holland. There's a station near the holiday centre. And actually there's a direct coach … we could take that from the port …

Girl: Yeah, Dad, but we'll want to get out and about, won't we? Not spend all our time in the centre …

Father: Yep, you're right. We'll stick to my original idea.

Girl: Good.

Reading and Use of English

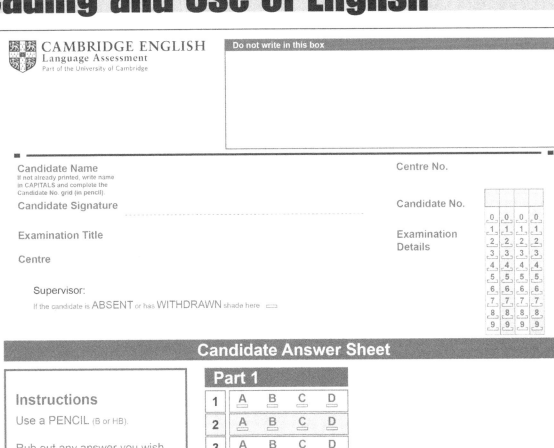

CAMBRIDGE ENGLISH
Language Assessment
Part of the University of Cambridge

Do not write in this box

Candidate Name
If not already printed, write name
in CAPITALS and complete the
Candidate No. grid (in pencil).

Candidate Signature

Examination Title

Centre

Supervisor:
If the candidate is ABSENT or has WITHDRAWN shade here ⊂⊃

Centre No.

Candidate No.

Examination
Details

Candidate Answer Sheet

Instructions

Use a PENCIL (B or HB).

Rub out any answer you wish
to change using an eraser.

Parts 1, 5, 6 and 7:
Mark ONE letter for each
question.

For example, if you think **B** is the right
answer to the question, mark your
answer sheet like this:

Parts 2, 3 and 4:
Write your answer clearly
in CAPITAL LETTERS.

For Parts 2 and 3 write one letter
in each box. For example:

Part 1

1	A	B	C	D
2	A	B	C	D
3	A	B	C	D
4	A	B	C	D
5	A	B	C	D
6	A	B	C	D
7	A	B	C	D
8	A	B	C	D

Part 2

Do not write
below here

9		1 0 u
10		1 0 u
11		1 0 u
12		1 0 u
13		1 0 u
14		1 0 u
15		1 0 u
16		1 0 u

Continues over ➜

Reading and Use of English

Part 3

Do not write below here

17		17 1 0 u
18		18 1 0 u
19		19 1 0 u
20		20 1 0 u
21		21 1 0 u
22		22 1 0 u
23		23 1 0 u
24		24 1 0 u

Part 4

Do not write below here

25		25 2 1 0 u
26		26 2 1 0 u
27		27 2 1 0 u
28		28 2 1 0 u
29		29 2 1 0 u
30		30 2 1 0 u

Part 5

31	A B C D
32	A B C D
33	A B C D
34	A B C D
35	A B C D
36	A B C D

Part 6

37	A B C D E F G
38	A B C D E F G
39	A B C D E F G
40	A B C D E F G
41	A B C D E F G
42	A B C D E F G

Part 7

43	A B C D E F
44	A B C D E F
45	A B C D E F
46	A B C D E F
47	A B C D E F
48	A B C D E F
49	A B C D E F
50	A B C D E F
51	A B C D E F
52	A B C D E F

Listening

Part 1

	A	B	C
1	⊂⊃	⊂⊃	⊂⊃
2	⊂⊃	⊂⊃	⊂⊃
3	⊂⊃	⊂⊃	⊂⊃
4	⊂⊃	⊂⊃	⊂⊃
5	⊂⊃	⊂⊃	⊂⊃
6	⊂⊃	⊂⊃	⊂⊃
7	⊂⊃	⊂⊃	⊂⊃
8	⊂⊃	⊂⊃	⊂⊃

Part 2 (Remember to write in CAPITAL LETTERS or numbers)

Do not write below here

9		9 1 0 u
10		10 1 0 u
11		11 1 0 u
12		12 1 0 u
13		13 1 0 u
14		14 1 0 u
15		15 1 0 u
16		16 1 0 u
17		17 1 0 u
18		18 1 0 u

Part 3

	A	B	C	D	E	F	G	H
19	⊂⊃	⊂⊃	⊂⊃	⊂⊃	⊂⊃	⊂⊃	⊂⊃	⊂⊃
20	⊂⊃	⊂⊃	⊂⊃	⊂⊃	⊂⊃	⊂⊃	⊂⊃	⊂⊃
21	⊂⊃	⊂⊃	⊂⊃	⊂⊃	⊂⊃	⊂⊃	⊂⊃	⊂⊃
22	⊂⊃	⊂⊃	⊂⊃	⊂⊃	⊂⊃	⊂⊃	⊂⊃	⊂⊃
23	⊂⊃	⊂⊃	⊂⊃	⊂⊃	⊂⊃	⊂⊃	⊂⊃	⊂⊃

Part 4

	A	B	C
24	⊂⊃	⊂⊃	⊂⊃
25	⊂⊃	⊂⊃	⊂⊃
26	⊂⊃	⊂⊃	⊂⊃
27	⊂⊃	⊂⊃	⊂⊃
28	⊂⊃	⊂⊃	⊂⊃
29	⊂⊃	⊂⊃	⊂⊃
30	⊂⊃	⊂⊃	⊂⊃

Acknowledgements

Author acknowledgements

The authors would like to thank their editors, Judith Greet, Ann-Marie Murphy and Diane Hall, for their expertise and constant support. Many thanks also to Matt Stephens (production project manager), Chloe Szebrat (assistant permissions clearance controller), Louise Edgeworth (freelance picture researcher), Leon Chambers (audio producer), Sue Flood (proof reader)

Publisher acknowledgements

The authors and publishers are grateful to the following for reviewing the material during the development process:

Susan Obiglio: Argentina; Maria Christaki: Greece; Jane Hoatson, Jessica Smith, Catherine Toomey: Italy; Katherine Bilsborough, Laura Clyde: Spain; Ludmila Kozhevnikova: Russia; Bridget Bloom, Helen Chilton, Mark Fountain, Rebecca Raynes: UK.

Thanks are also due to the teachers who contributed to initial research in to this course. In Milan, Italy: Judith Axelby, Liane Hyde, Rachel Shields, Prof. Barbagallo, Prof. Marrali; in Turin: Prof. Cook, Prof. Dickens, Prof. Grasso, Prof. Zoppas; in Genova Prof. Lovati, Prof. Risso. In Poland: teachers at Empik, Warsaw Study Centre, Warsaw University, ZS UMK. In Spain: Keith Appleby, Vicante Ferarios Maroto, Nick Tunstall, Lisa Wotton. In Switzerland: Keith Dabourn, Ms Eigner, Amy Jost, Ueli Hepp, Lori Kaithen, Eveline Reichel, Lee Walker and teachers at Berlitz, Berufschule Bulach, Sprachschule Schneiner, Liz and Michelle from the apprenticeship school.

Development of this publication has made use of the Cambridge English Corpus (CEC). The CEC is a computer database of contemporary spoken and written English, which currently stands at over one billion words. It includes British English, American English and other varieties of English. It also includes the Cambridge Learner Corpus, developed in collaboration with the University of Cambridge ESOL Examinations. Cambridge University Press has built up the CEC to provide evidence about language use that helps to produce better language teaching materials.

This product is informed by the English Vocabulary Profile, built as part of English Profile, a collaborative programme designed to enhance the learning, teaching and assessment of English worldwide. Its main funding partners are Cambridge University Press and Cambridge ESOL and its aim is to create a 'profile' for English linked to the Common European Framework of Reference for Languages (CEFR). English Profile outcomes, such as the English Vocabulary Profile, will provide detailed information about the language that learners can be expected to demonstrate at each CEFR level, offering a clear benchmark for learners' proficiency. For more information, please visit www.englishprofile.org

Photo acknowledgements

The authors and publishers acknowledge the following sources of copyright material and are grateful for the permissions granted. While every effort has been made, it has not always been possible to identify the sources of all the material used, or to trace all copyright holders. If any omissions are brought to our notice, we will be happy to include the appropriate acknowledgements on reprinting.

The publishers are grateful to the following for permission to reproduce copyright photographs and material:

T = Top, C = Centre, B = Below, L = Left, R = Right, B/G = background
p. 9(TL): Thinkstock/David De Lossy; p. 9(C): Fotolia/Mr Markin; p. 9(TR): istockphoto/Alija; p. 9(BR): Thorpe Park; Corbis/Images Source; p. 33(TL): Alamy/Ashley Cooper Pics; p. 33(TR): Glowimages/Cultura; p. 33(BR): vThinkstock/Digital Vision; p. 33(BR): Getty Images/DreamPictures; p. 42(T): Getty Images/ Picturenet; p. 42(CT): Alamy/Justin Kasez08z; p. 42(CB): Alamy/David J Green-Lifestyle themes; p. 42(B): Superstock/ICP/age footstock.

Illustrations by:
p. 21: John Batten (Beehive illustrations).

Design, layout and art edited by Wild Apple Design Ltd.